COLORING
MANDALAS

FOR THE HEART, SOUL AND MIND

MOTIVATING AND INSPIRING DESIGNS

MARGGIORI LOPEZ

All rights reserved.
No part of this publication may be copied reproduced in any format, by any means, electronic or otherwise without prior consent from the copyright owner and publisher of this book.

Welcome to this motivating and inspiring coloring book!

We would love to see your masterpieces! Share your artwork by tagging us @Motivating.Mandalas and using the hashtag #MotivatingMandala

We donate 21% of sales to charity for children in need of physical therapy, children's education, and victims of domestic abuse.

We kindly ask you to please leave us a positive review

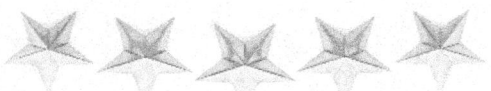

This coloring book is dedicated to
Leonardo, Cayden, Johan, Aguacate,
Blake, and Keanu.

May your lives be filled with all the
colors of the universe.

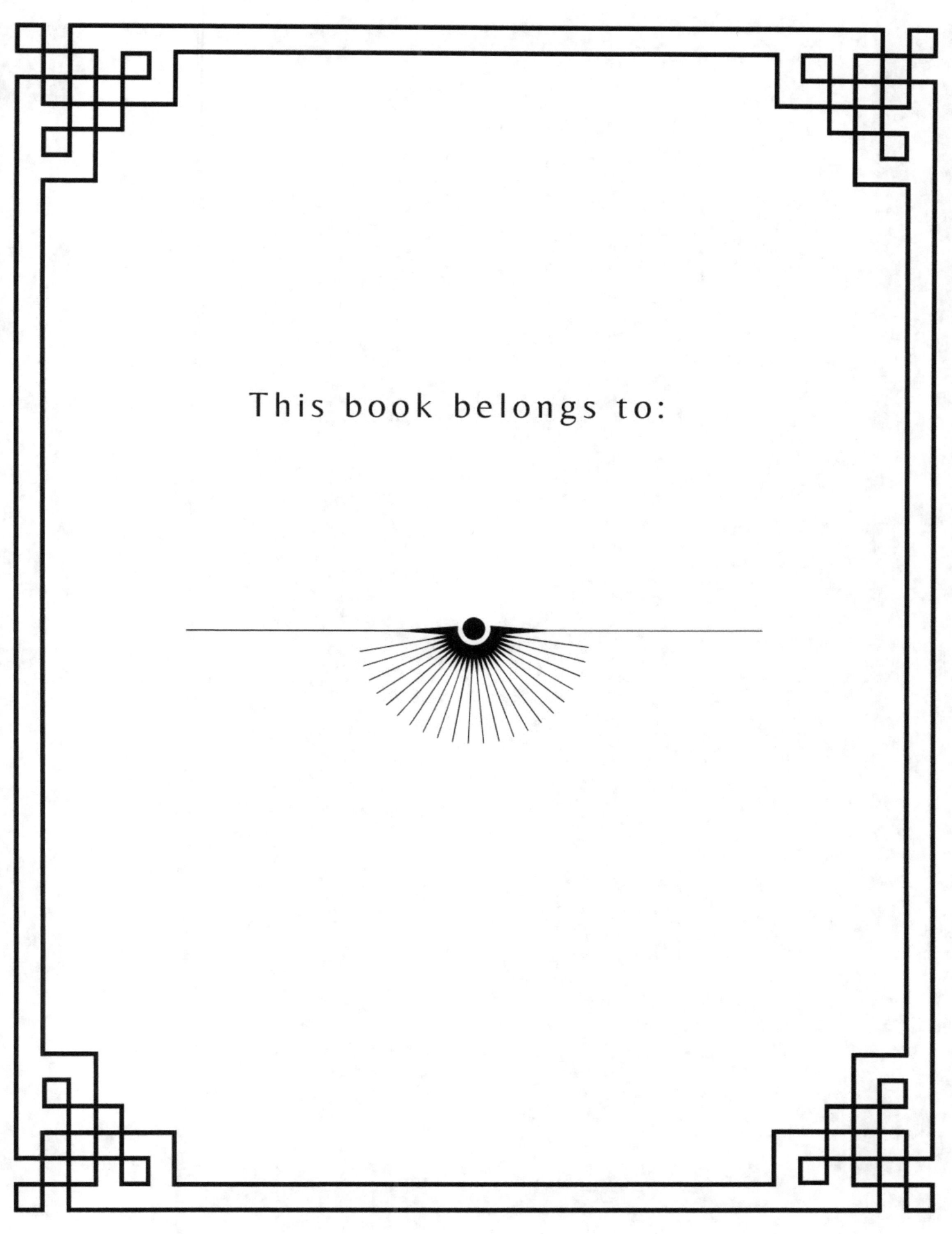

This book belongs to:

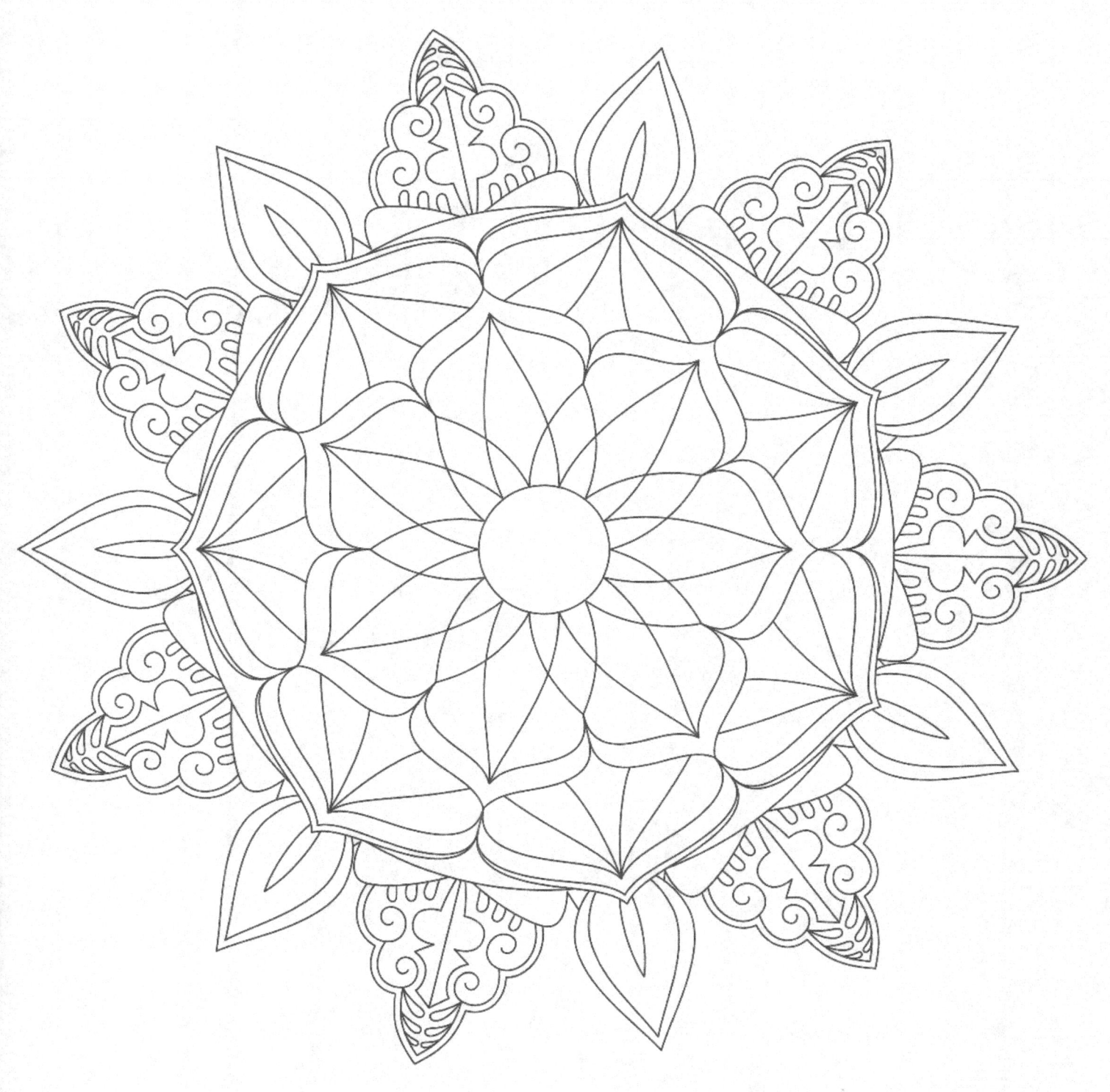

"You're off to great places, today is your day. Your mountain is waiting, so get on your way."
Dr. SeussAuthor

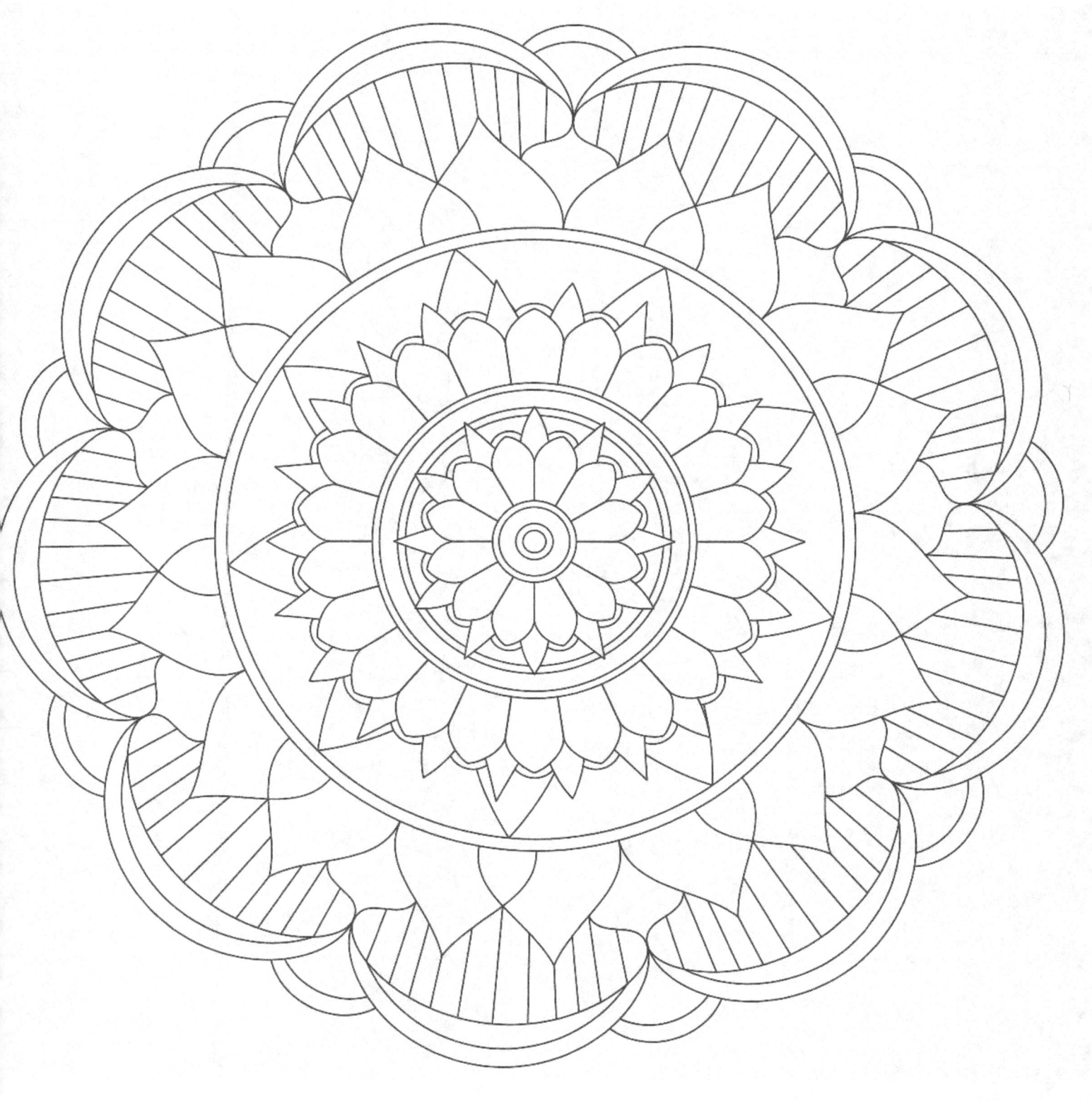

"You always pass failure on the way to success."
Mickey Rooney

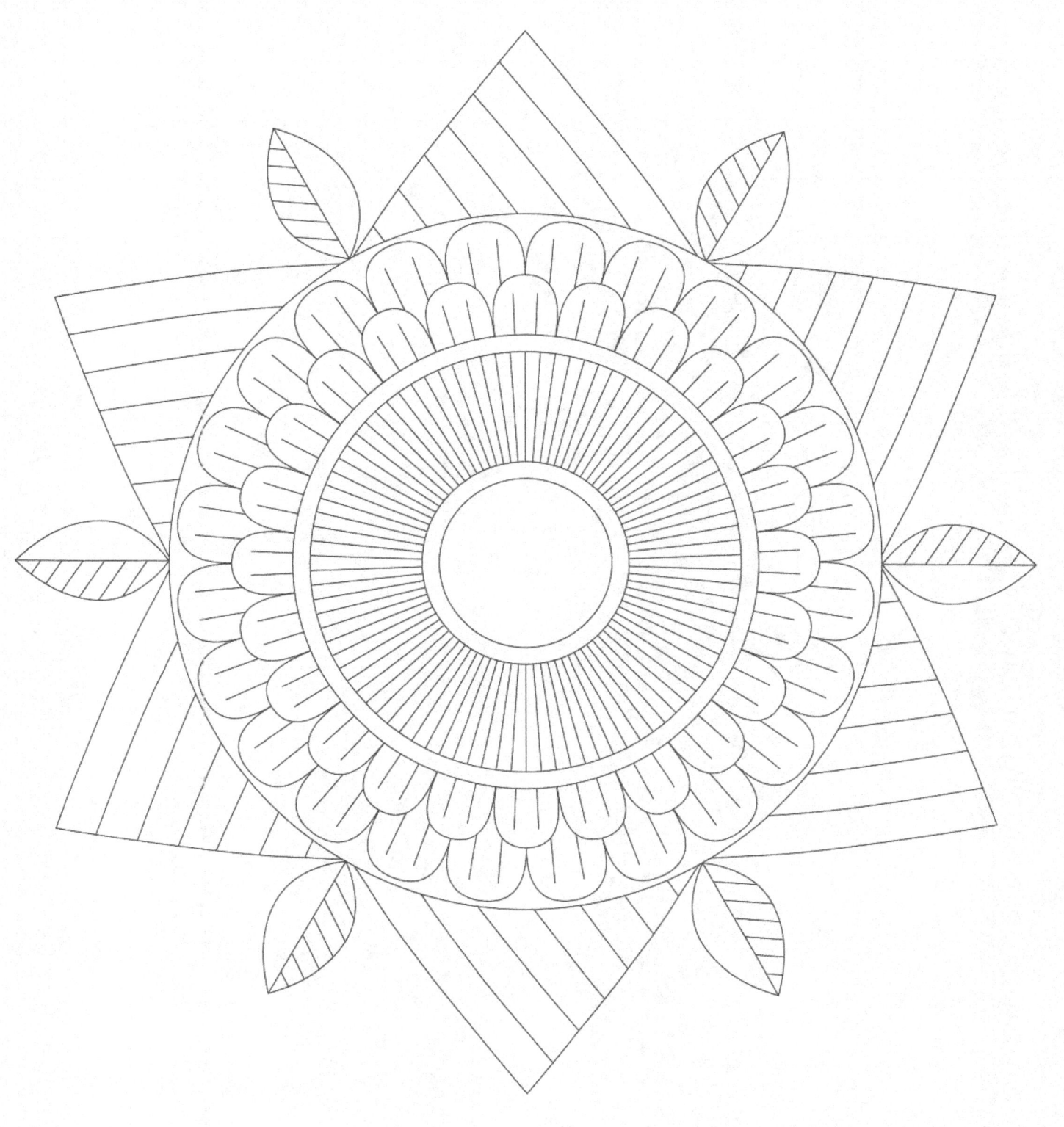

"No one is perfect - that's why pencils have erasers."
Wolfgang Riebe

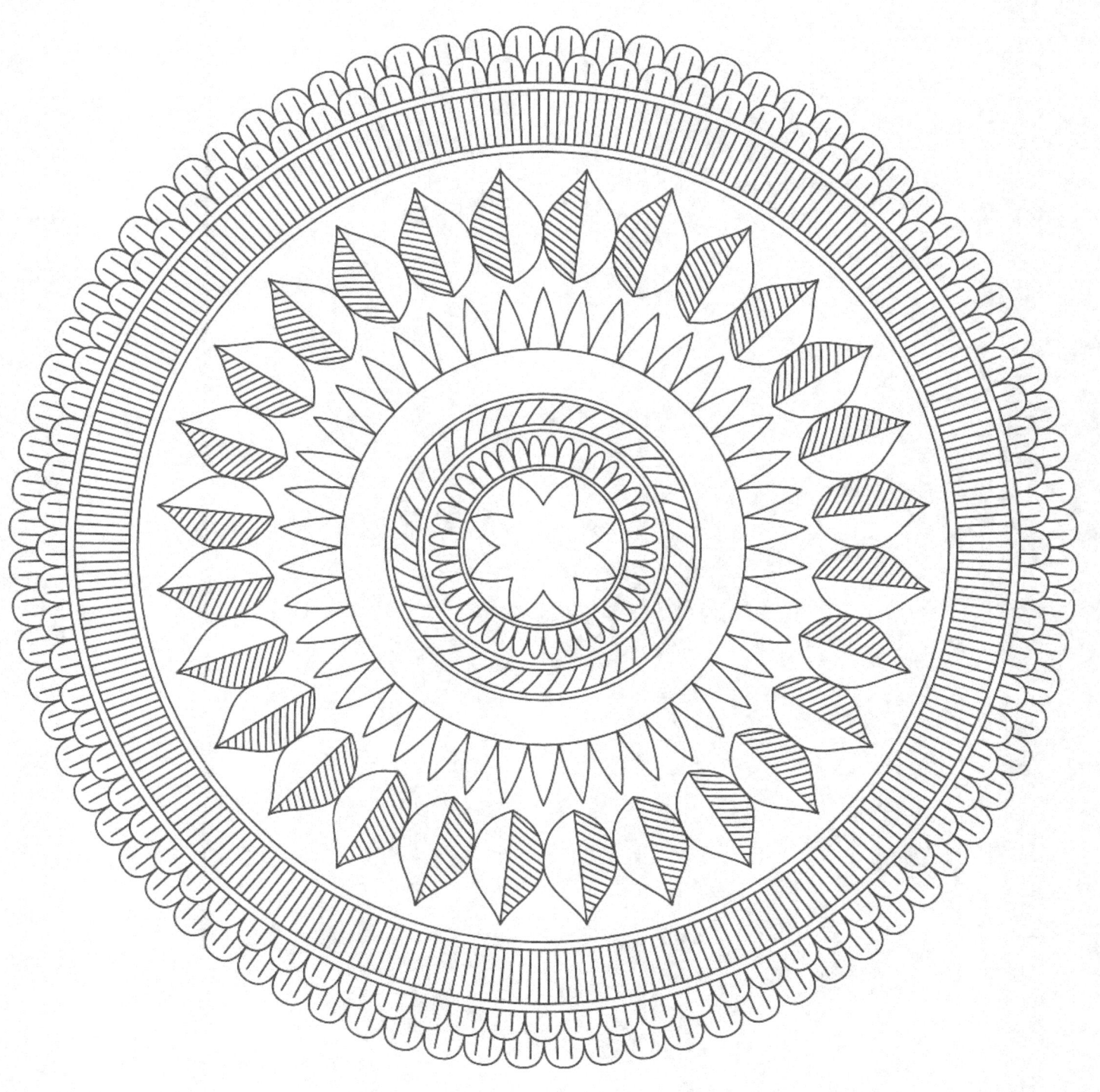

"Winning doesn't always mean being first.
Winning means you're doing better than
you've done before."
Bonnie Blair

"You're braver than you believe and stronger than you seem, and smarter than you think."
A.A. Mine

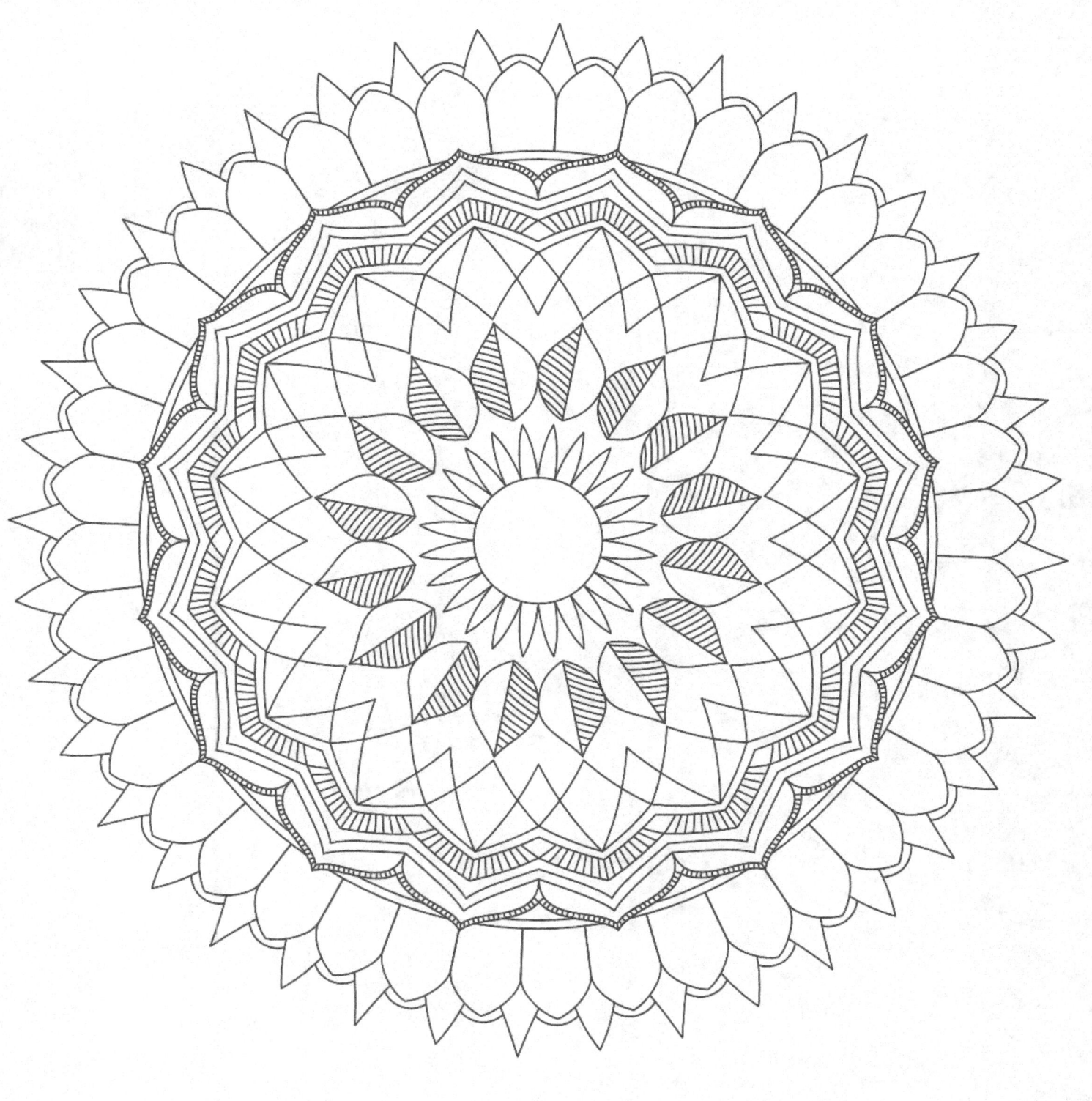

"It always seems impossible until it is done."
Nelson Mandela

"Keep your face to the sunshine and you cannot see a shadow."
Helen Keller

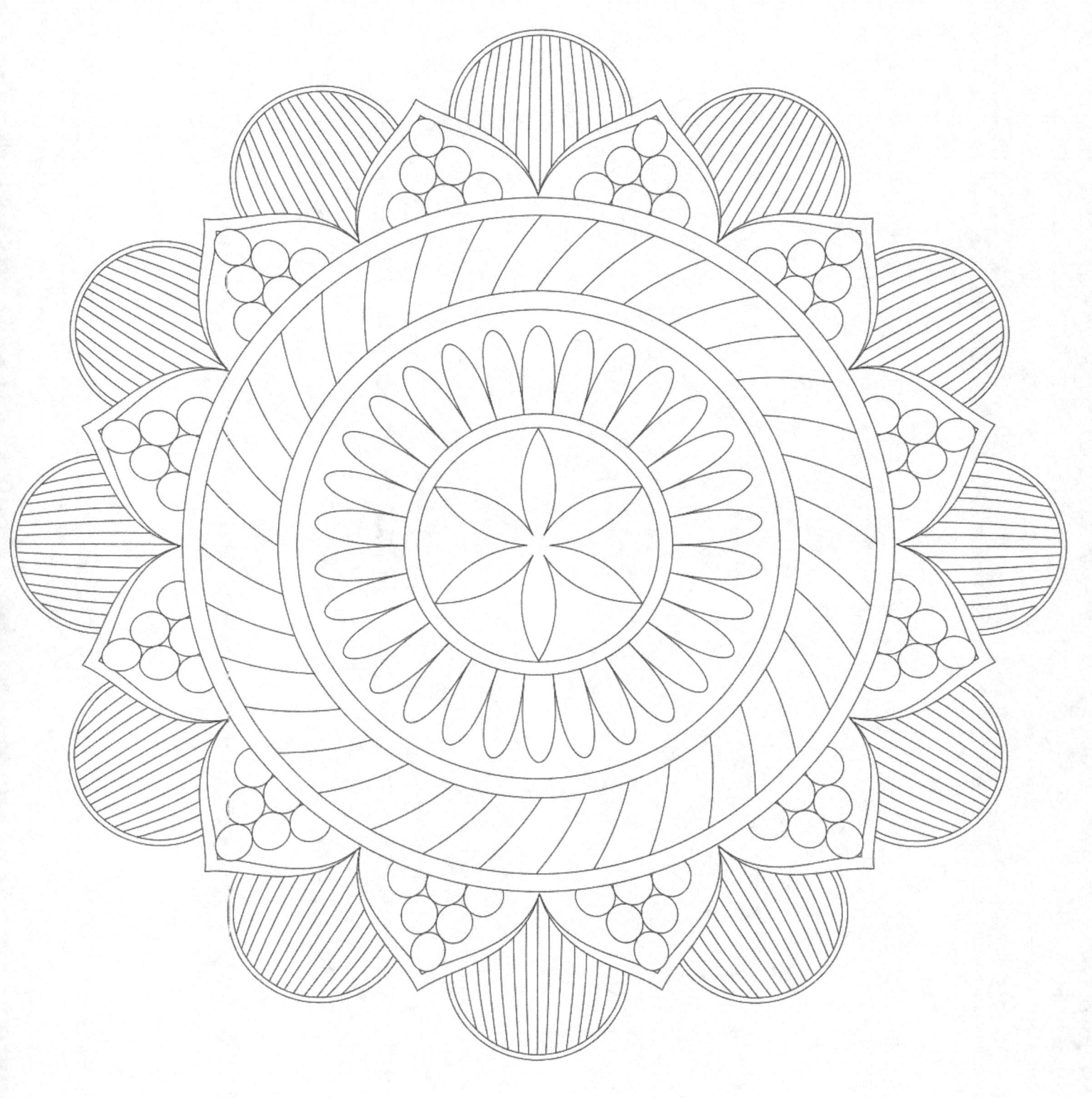

"Once you replace negative thoughts with positive ones, you'll start having positive results."
Willie Nelson

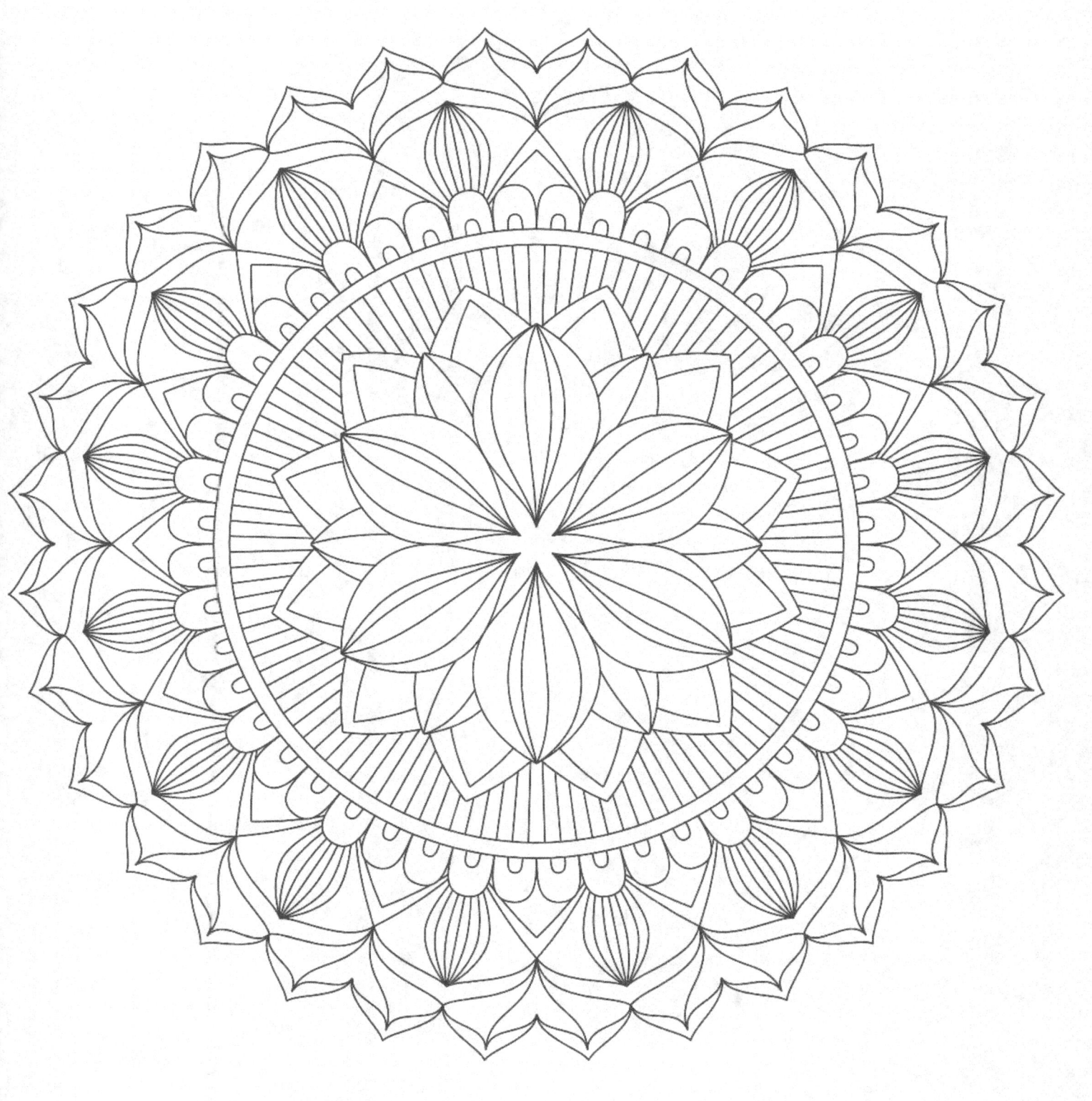

"Positive thinking will let you do everything better than negative thinking will."
Zig Ziglar

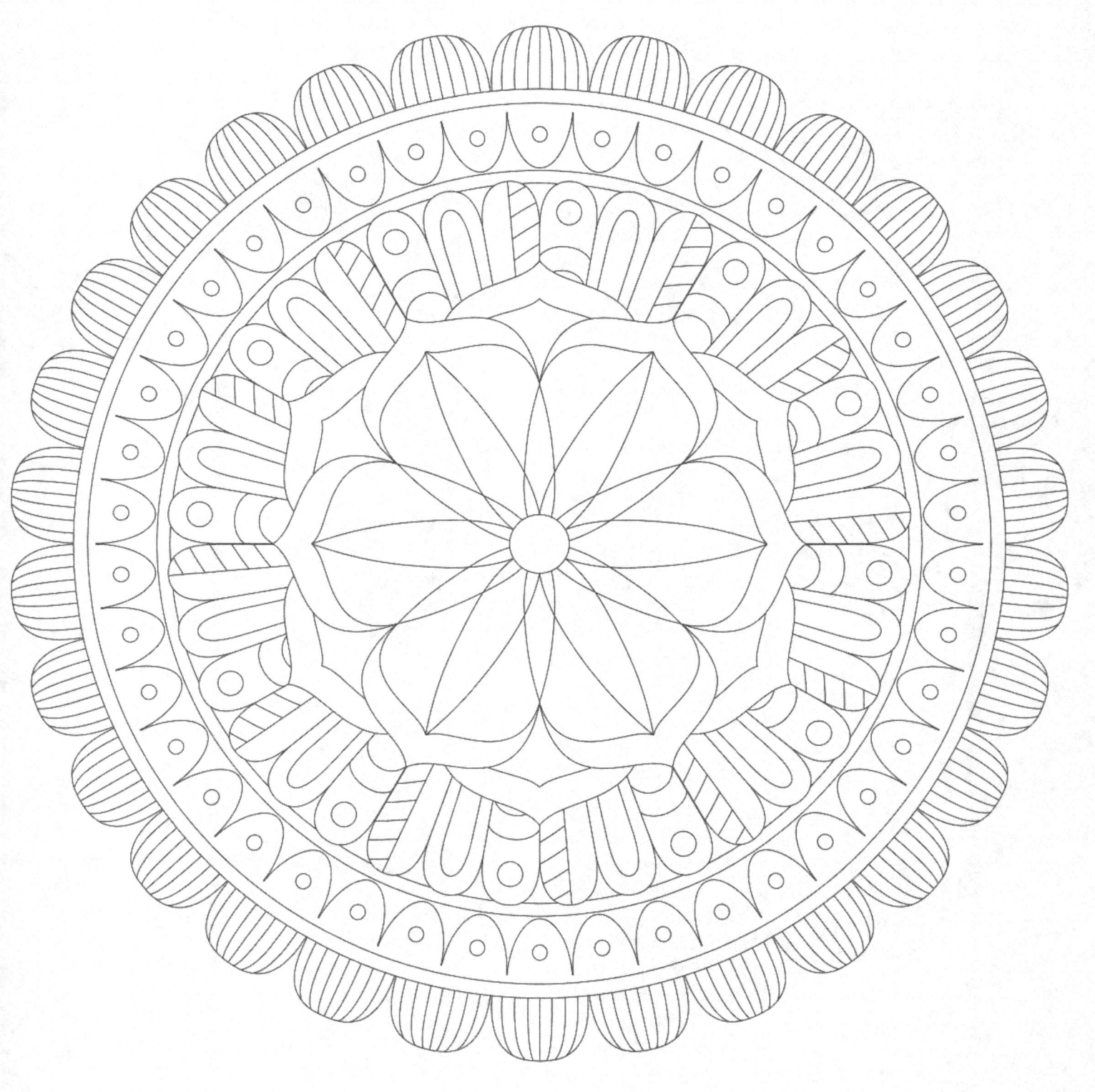

"In every day, there are 1,440 minutes. That means we have 1,440 daily opportunities to make a positive impact."
Les Brown

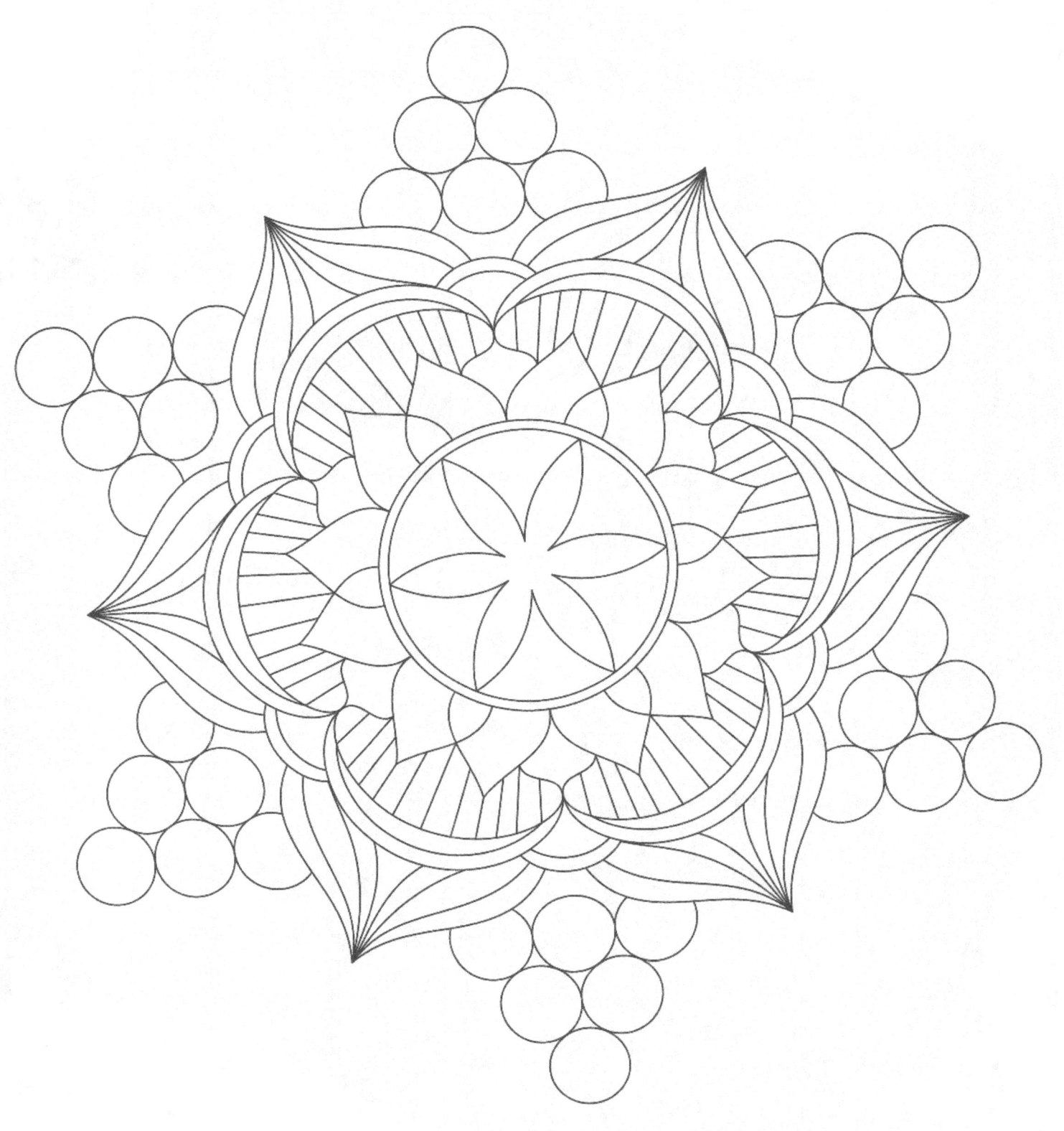

The only time you fail is when you fall down and stay down."
Stephen Richards

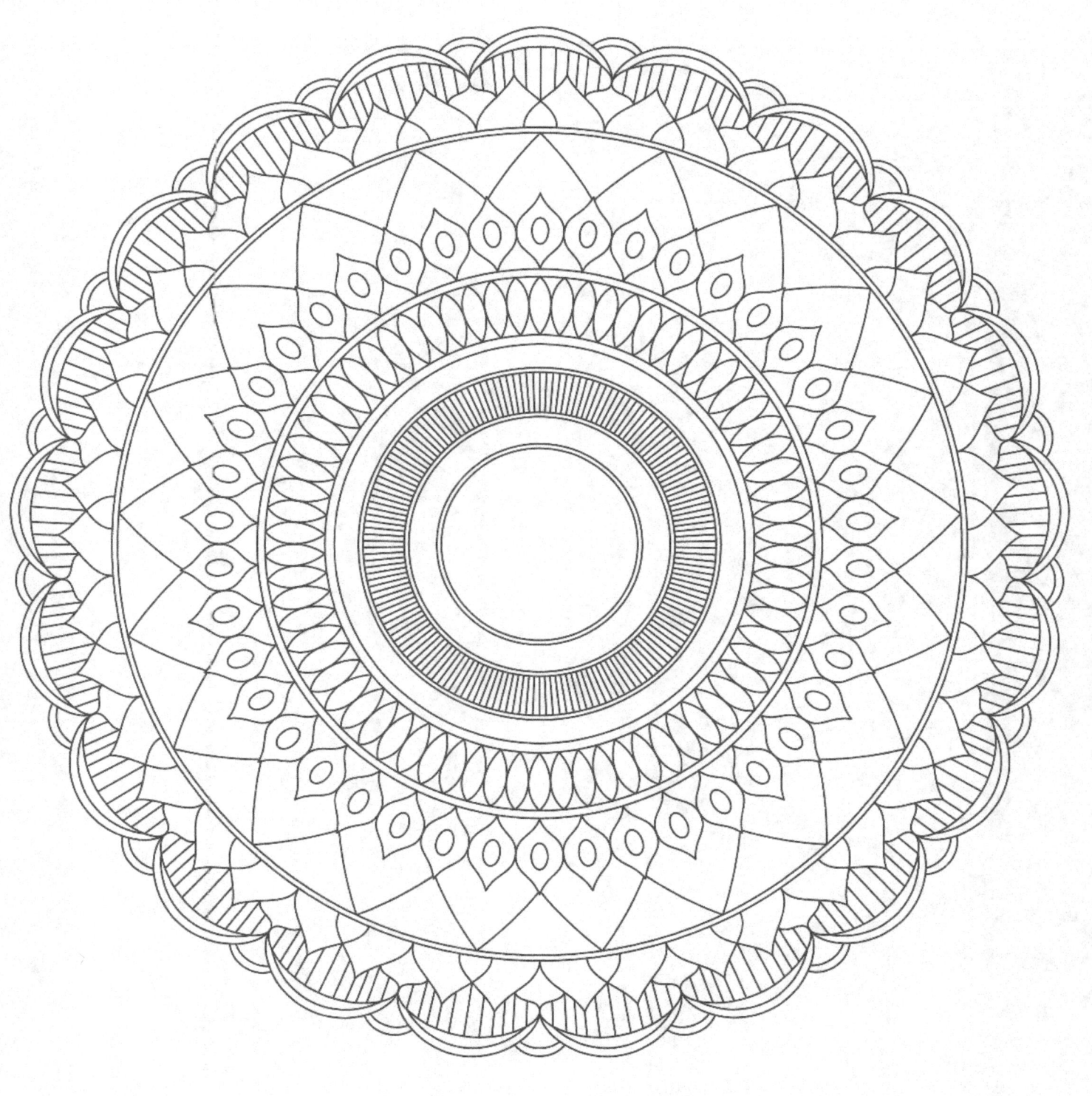

"When you are enthusiastic about what you do, you feel this positive energy. It's very simple."
Paulo Coelho

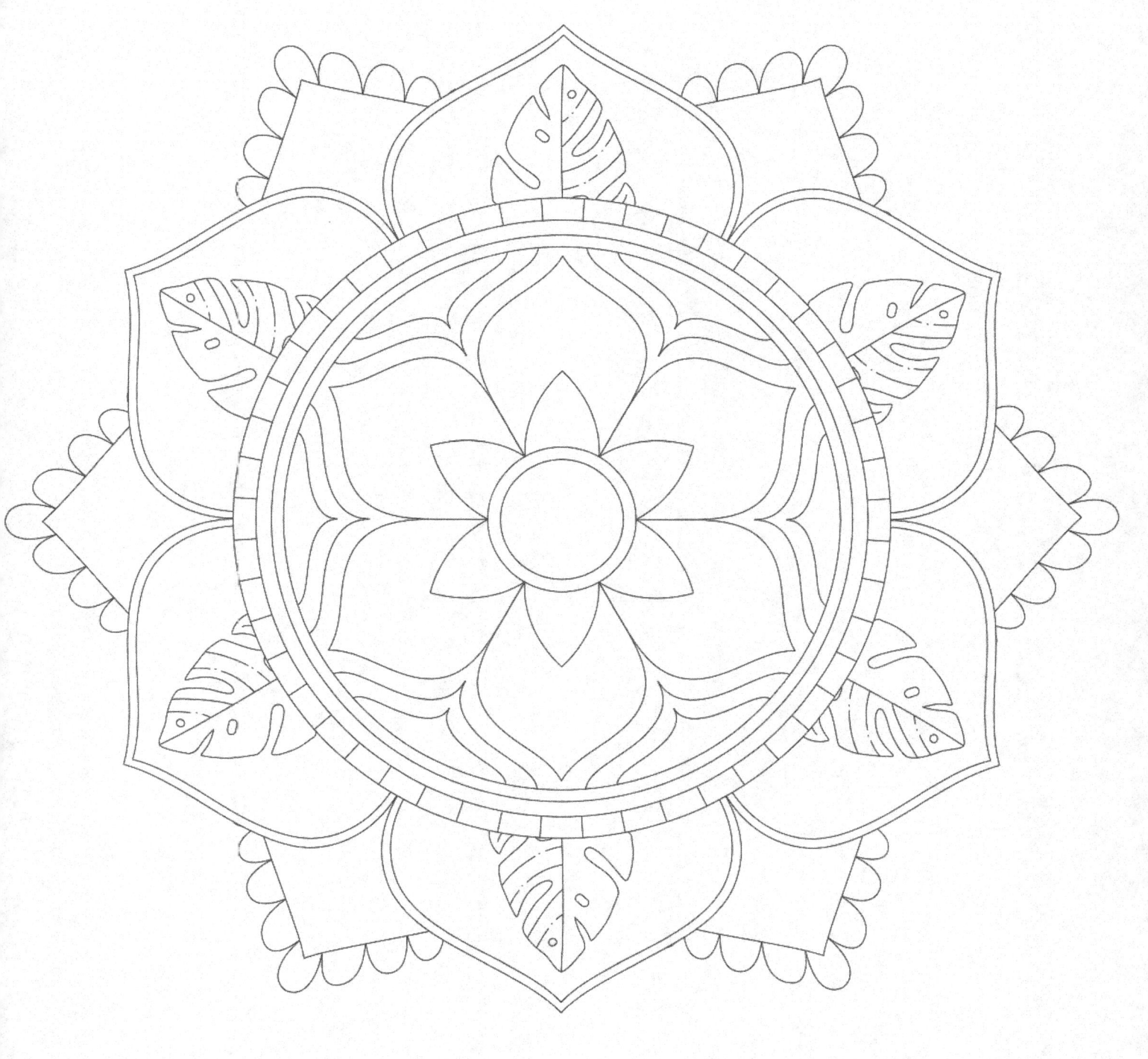

"Positive anything is better than negative nothing."
Elbert Hubbard

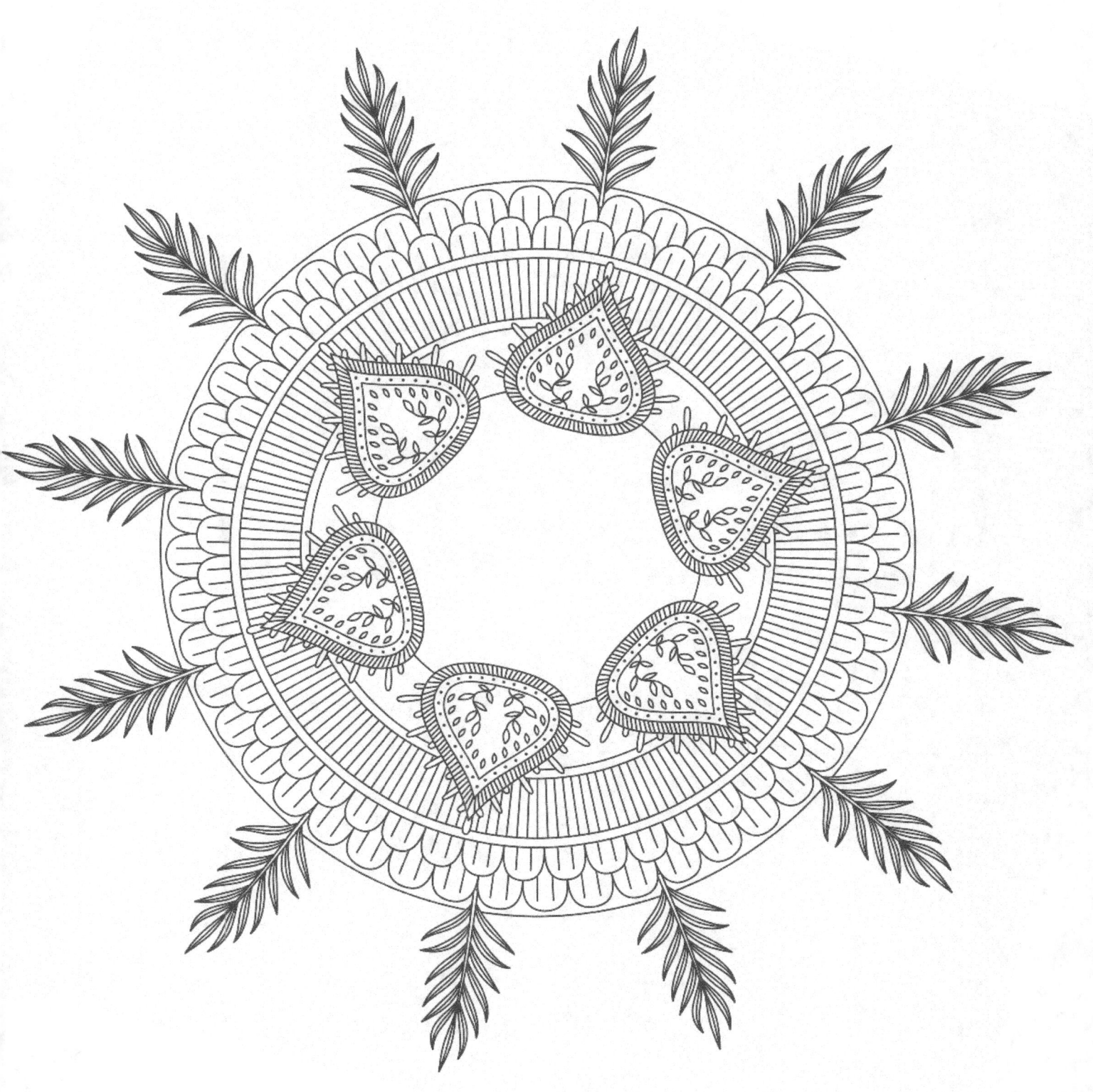

"Winning is fun, but those moments that you can touch someone's life in a very positive way are better."
Tim Howard

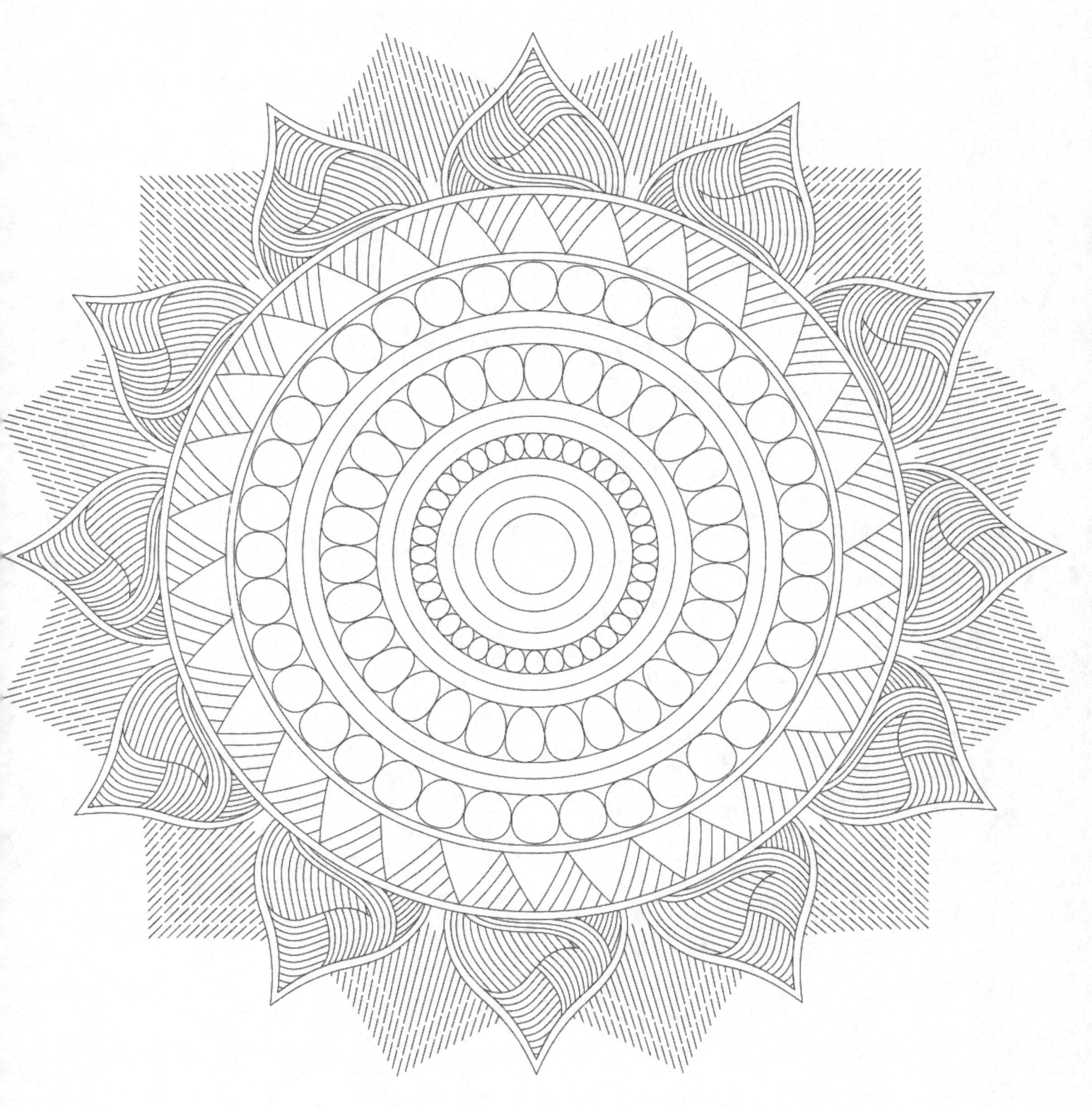

"Virtually nothing is impossible in this world if you just put your mind to it and maintain a positive attitude."
Lou Holtz

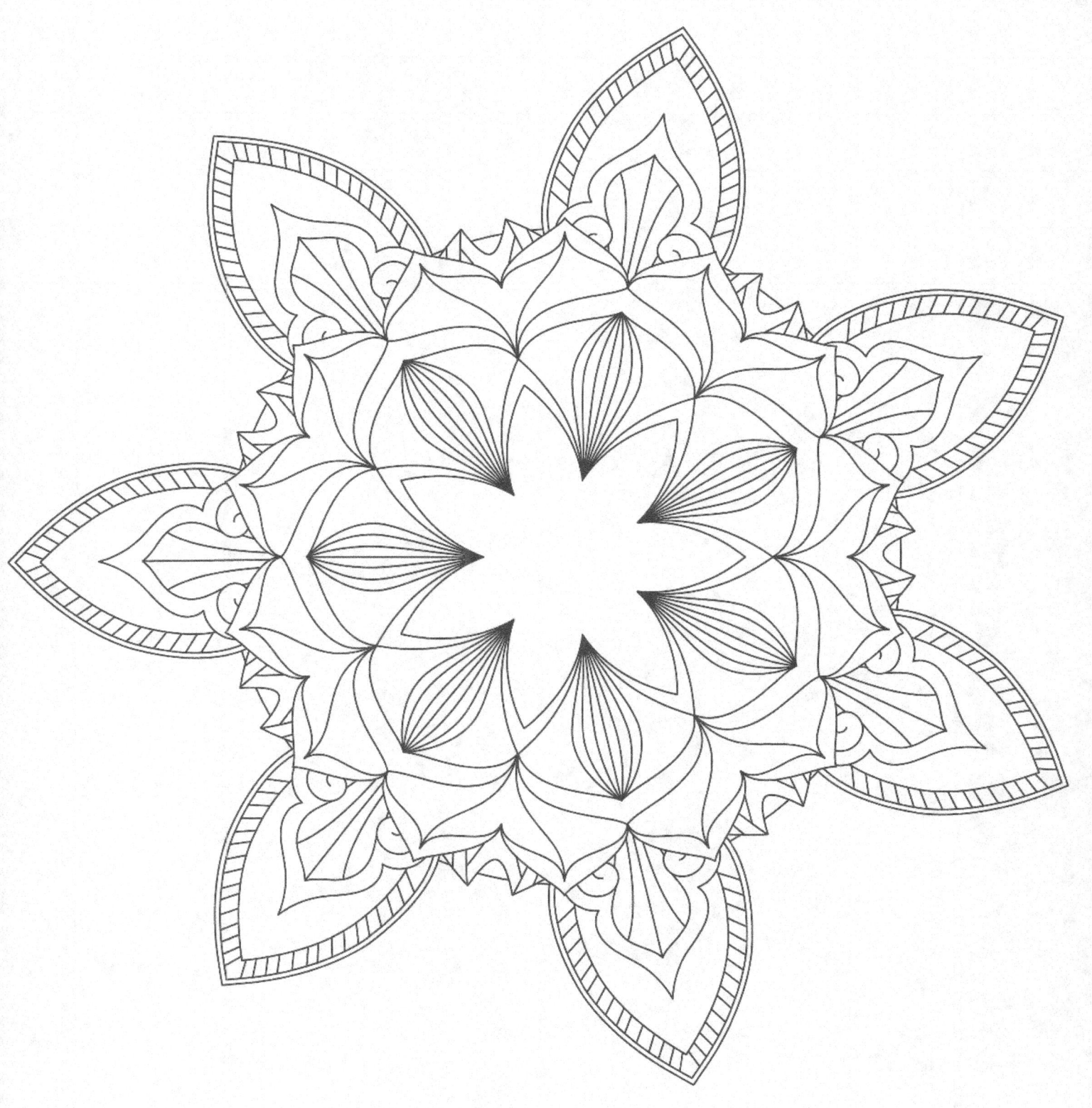

"Optimism is a happiness magnet. If you stay positive good things and good people will be drawn to you."
Mary Lou Retton

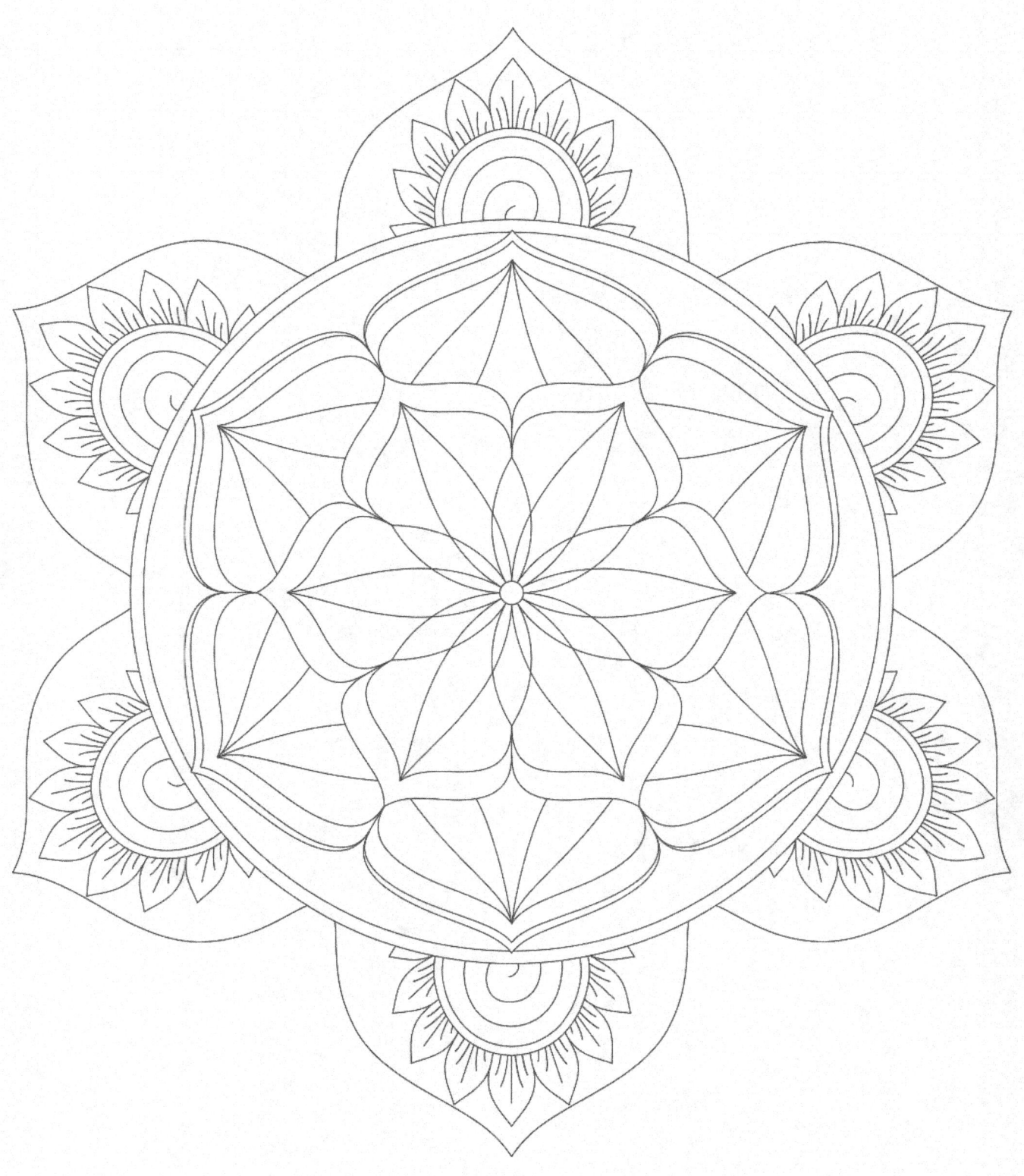

"It makes a big difference in your life when you stay positive."
Ellen DeGeneres

"If opportunity doesn't knock, build a door."
Milton Berle

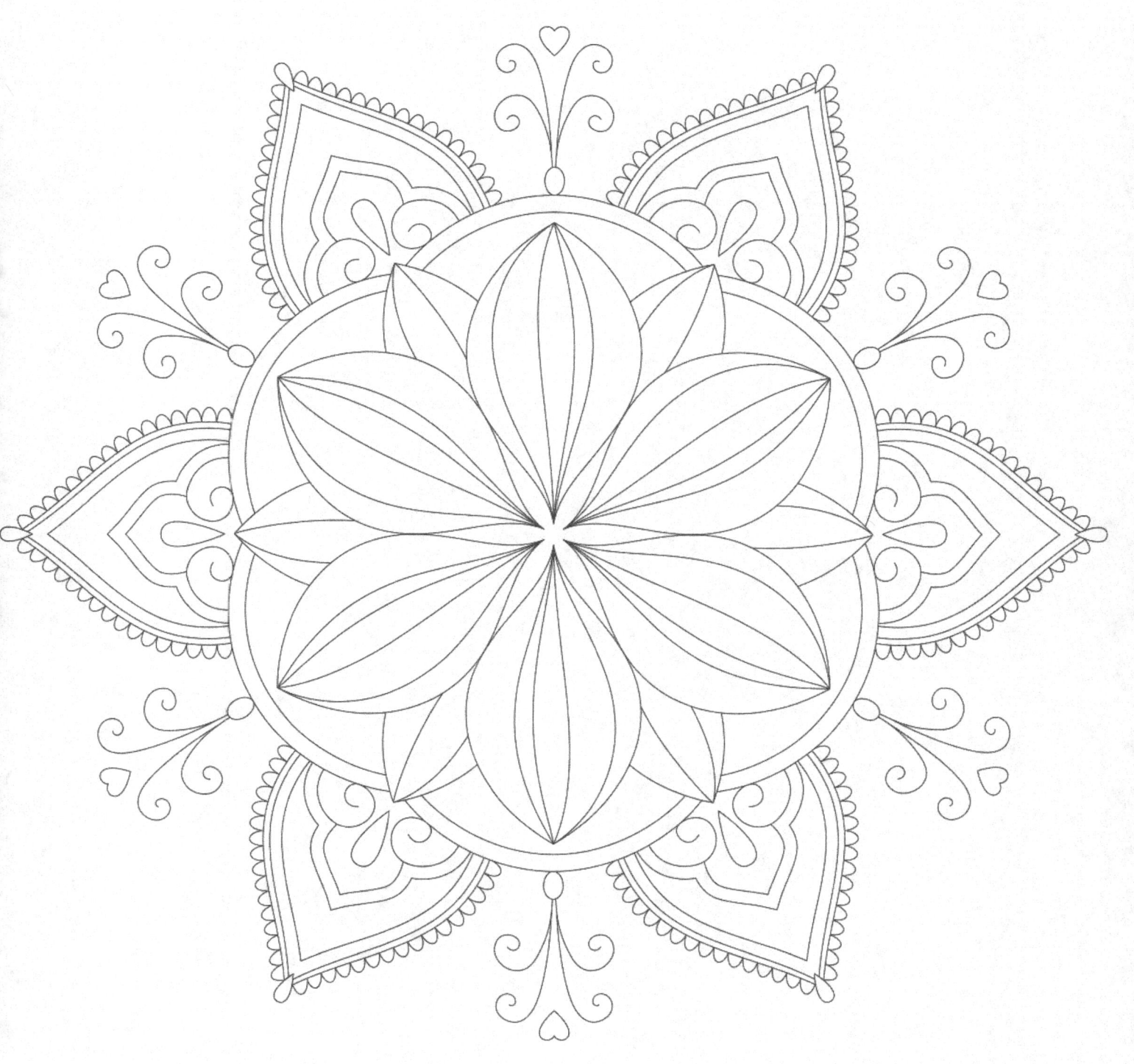

"Happiness is an attitude. We either make ourselves miserable, or happy and strong. The amount of work is the same."
Francesca Reigler

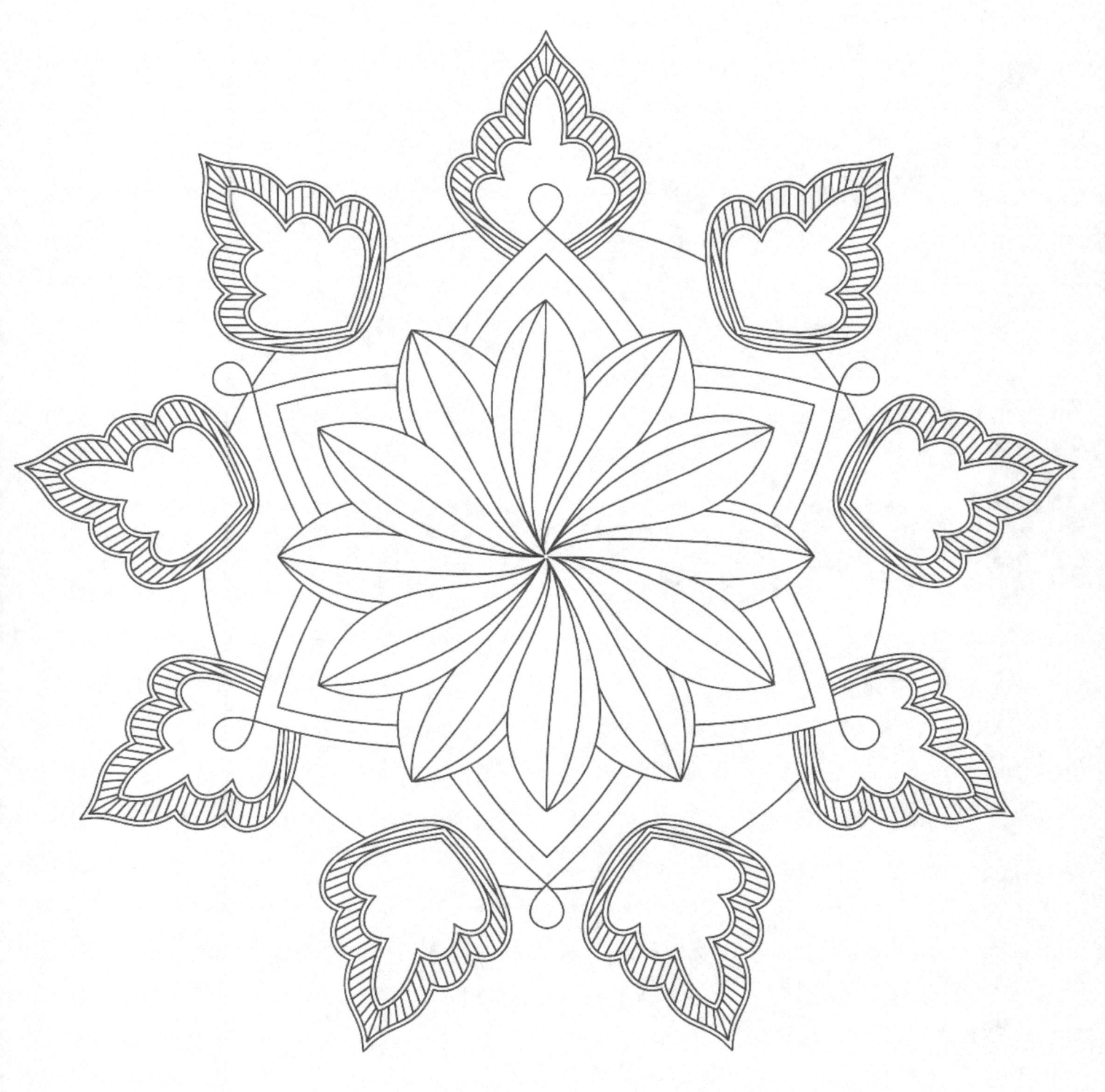

"You are never too old to set another goal or dream a new dream."
Les Brown

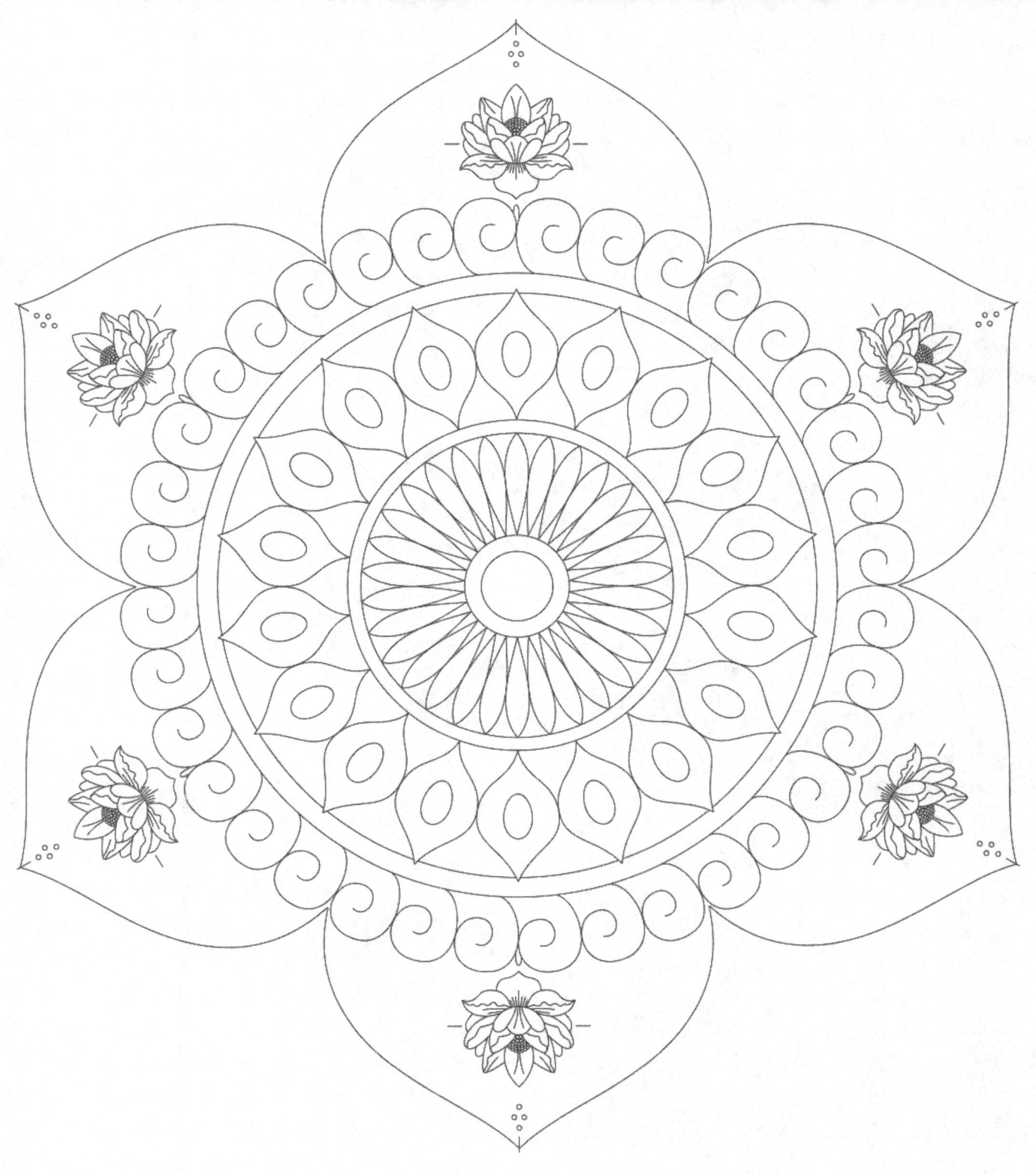

"The sun himself is weak when he first rises and gathers strength and courage as the day gets on."
Charles Dickens

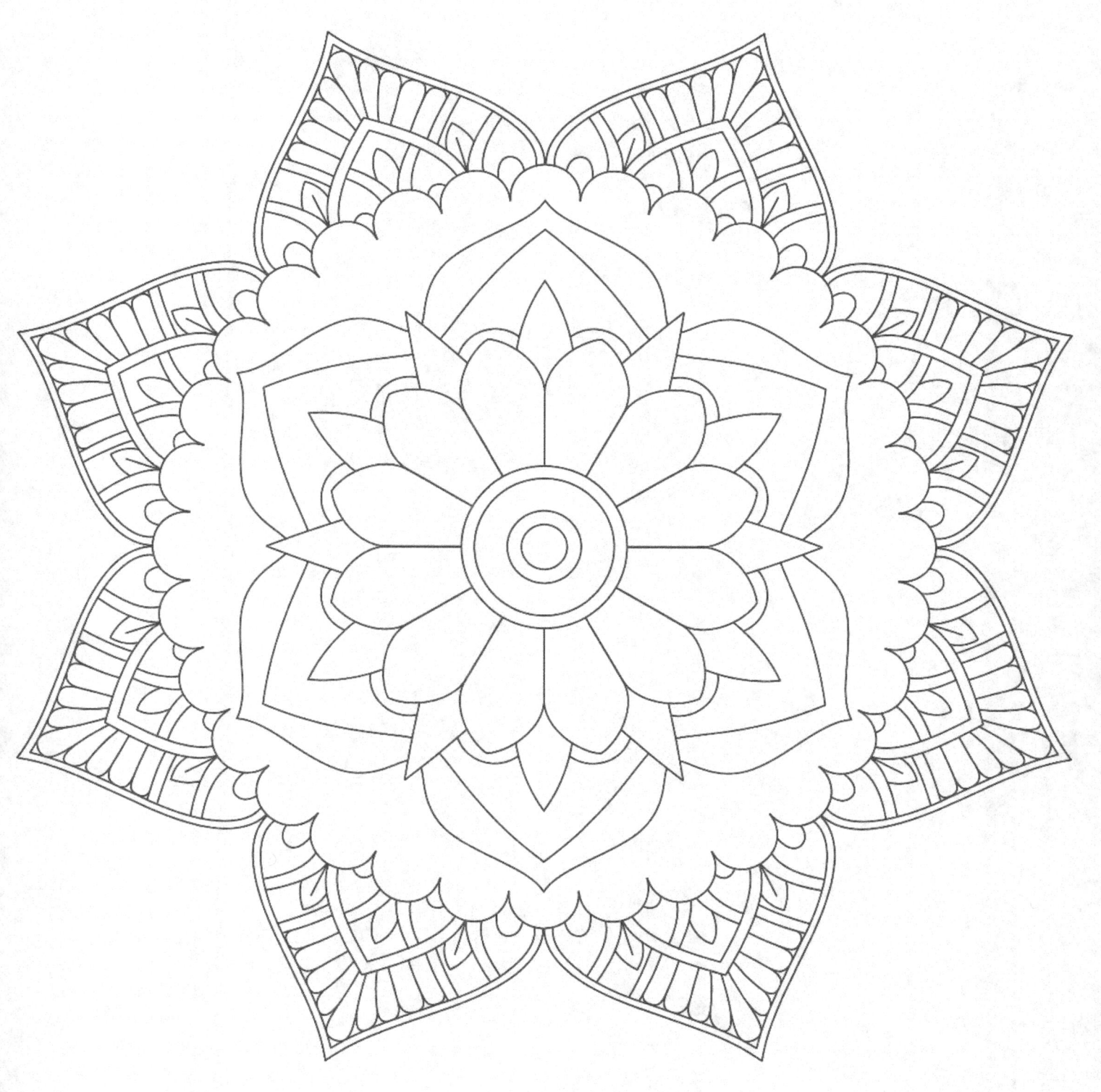

"It's not whether you get knocked down,
it's whether you get up."
Vince Lombardi

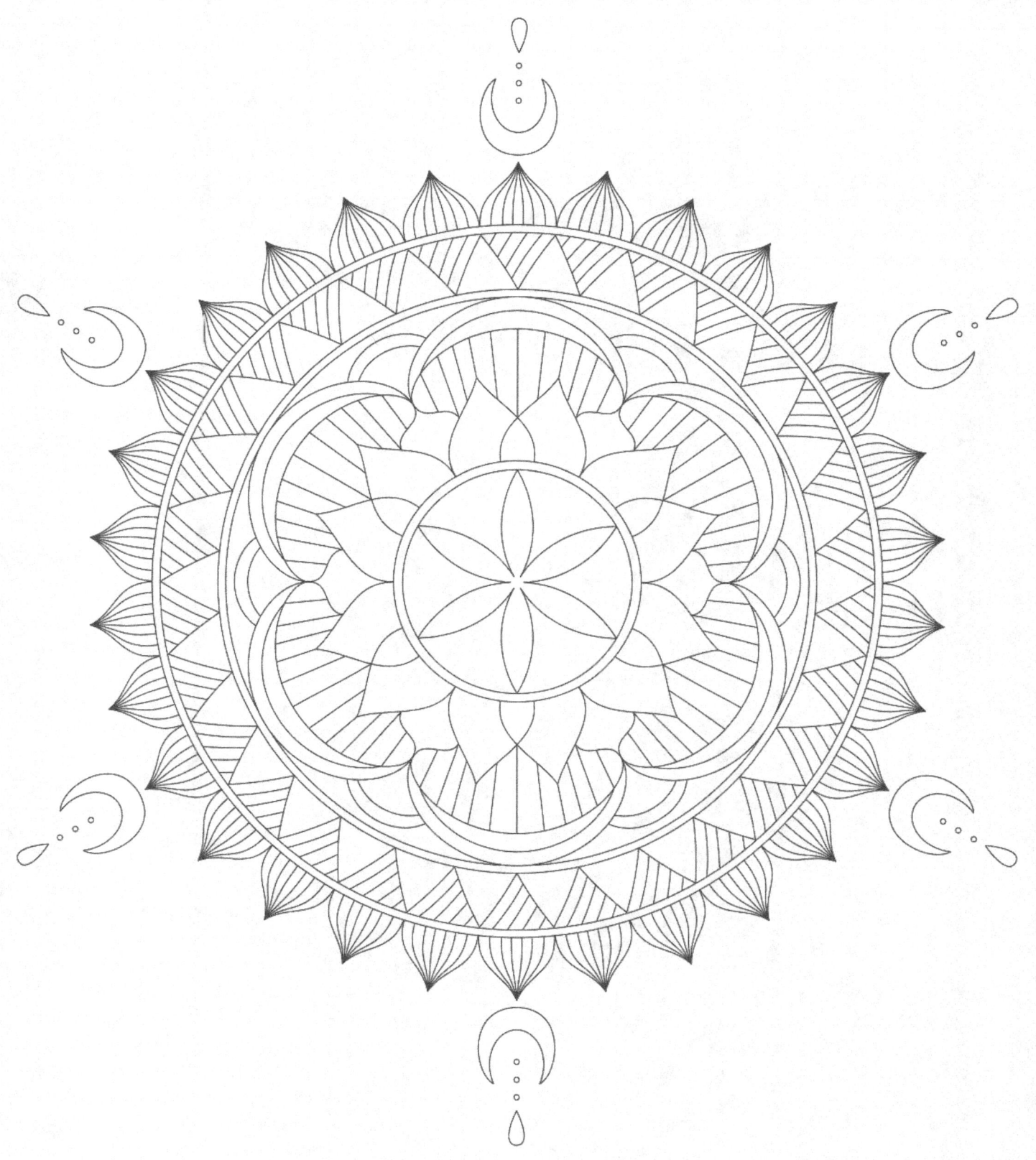

"The way I see it, if you want the rainbow,
you gotta put up with the rain."
Dolly Parton

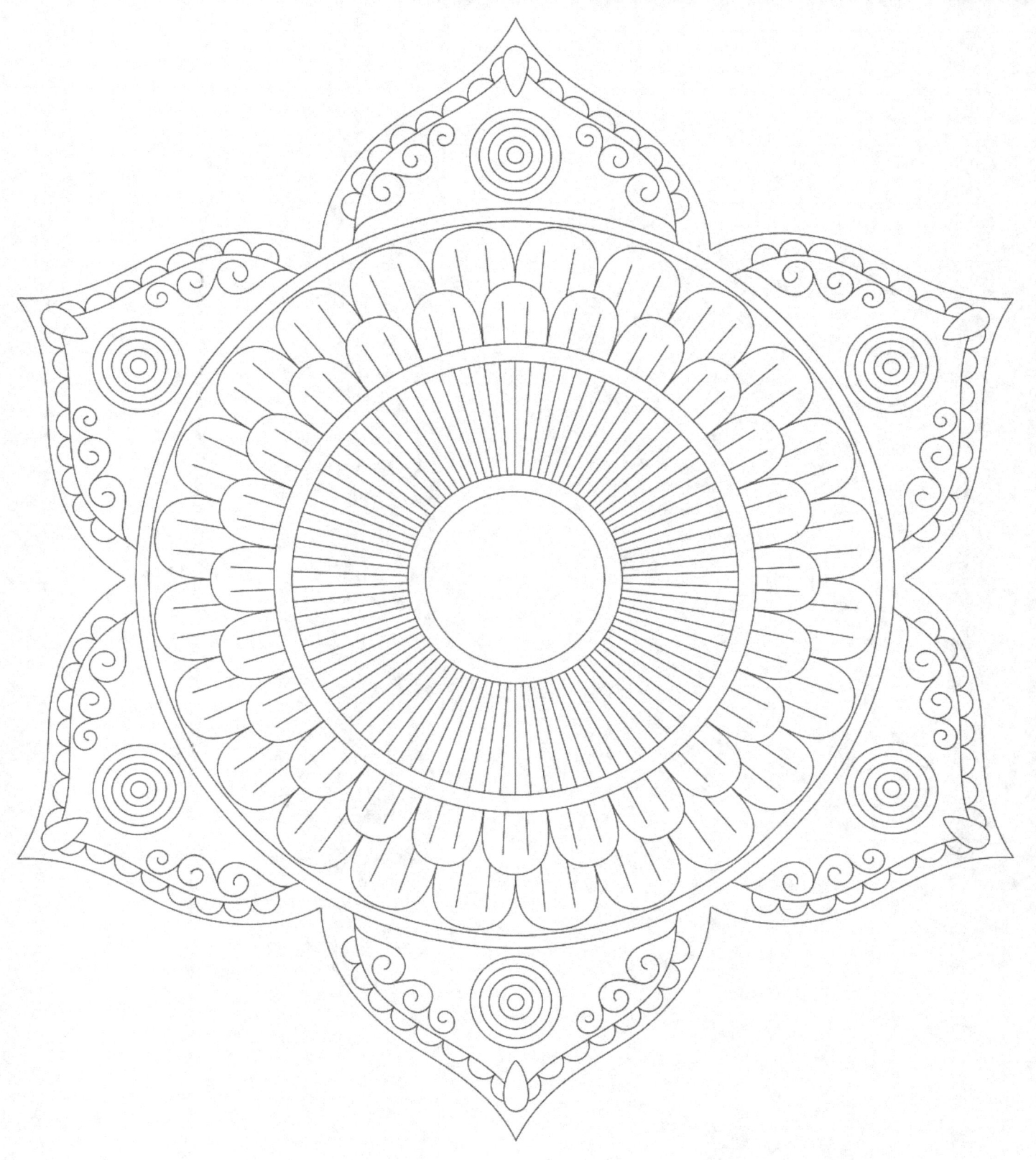

"The struggle you're in today is developing the strength youneed tomorrow."
Robert Tew

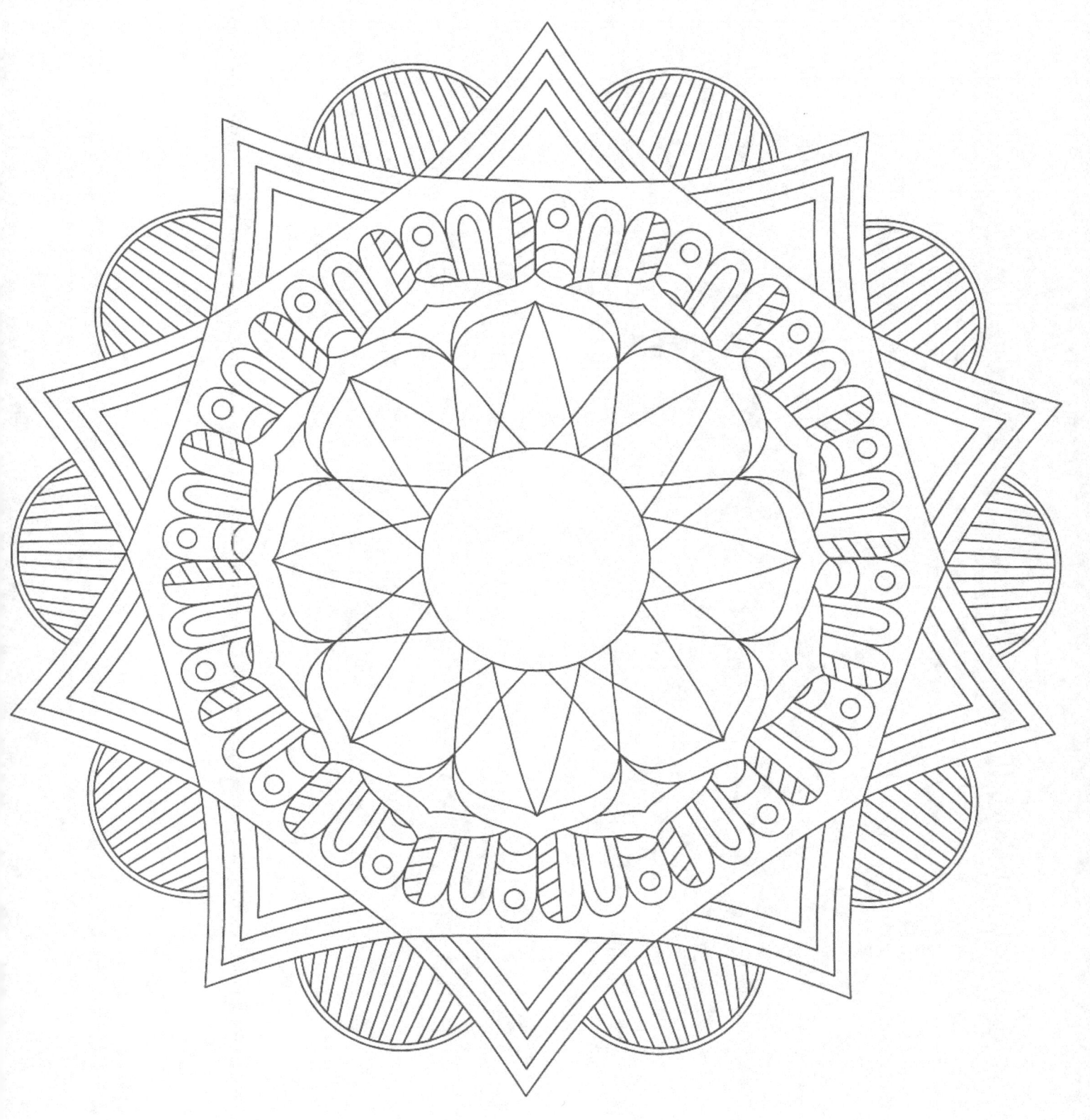

"Every day may not be good... but there's something good in every day."
Alice Morse Earle

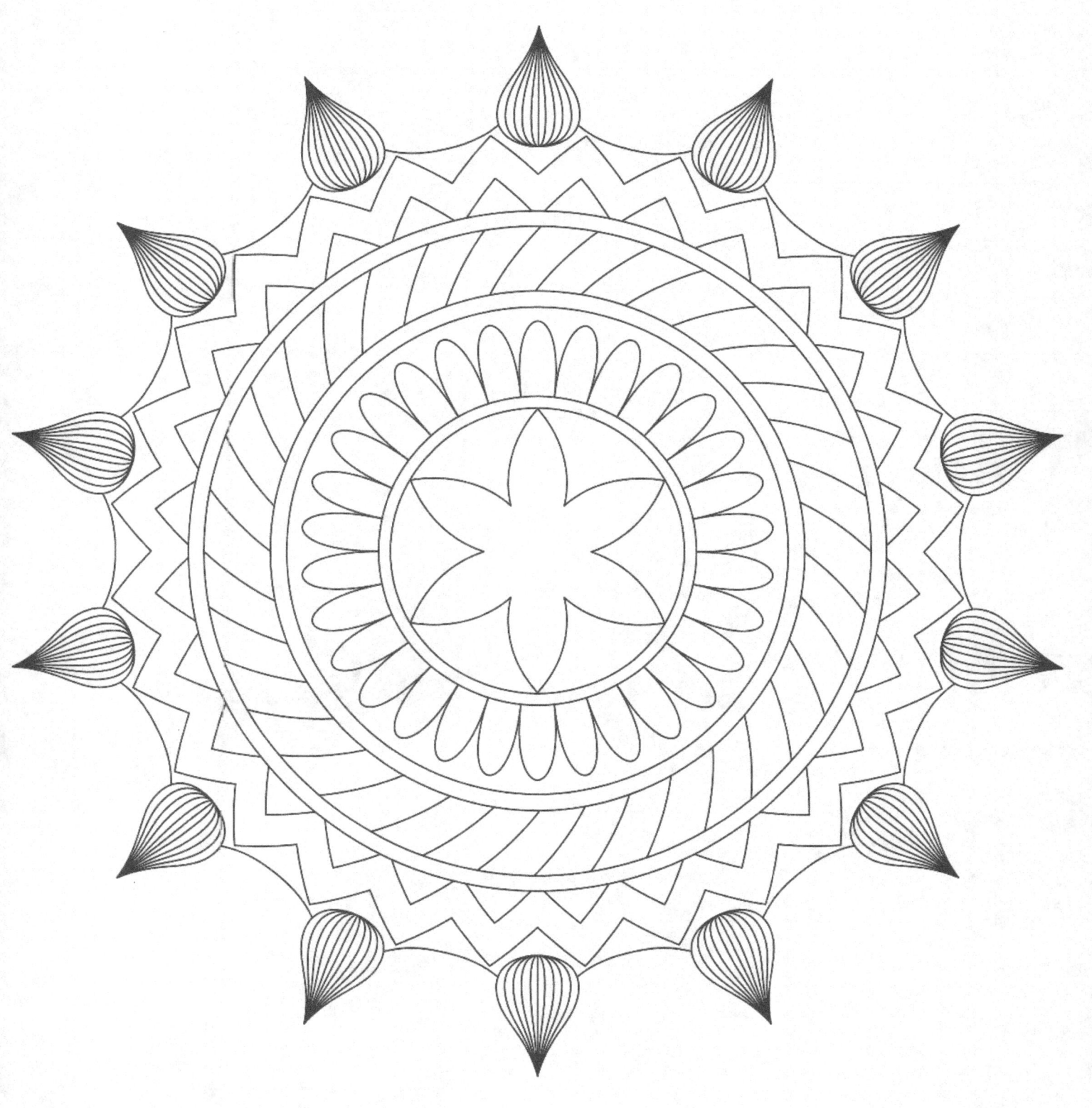

"The more you praise and celebrate your life, the more there is in life to celebrate."
Oprah Winfrey

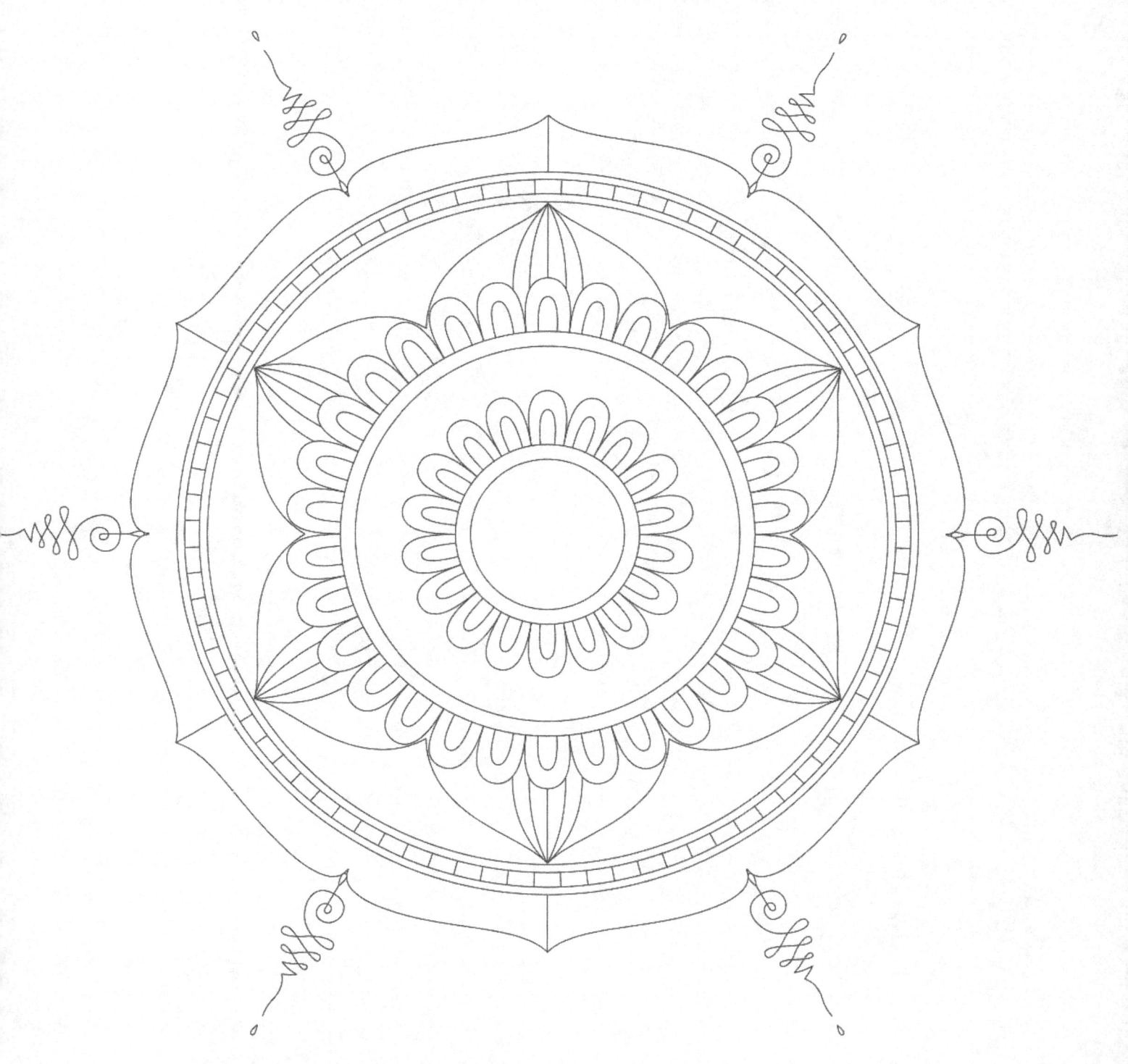

"Hard work keeps the wrinkles out of the
mind and spirit."
Helena Rubinstein

"The difference between ordinary and extraordinary is that little extra."
Jimmy Johnson

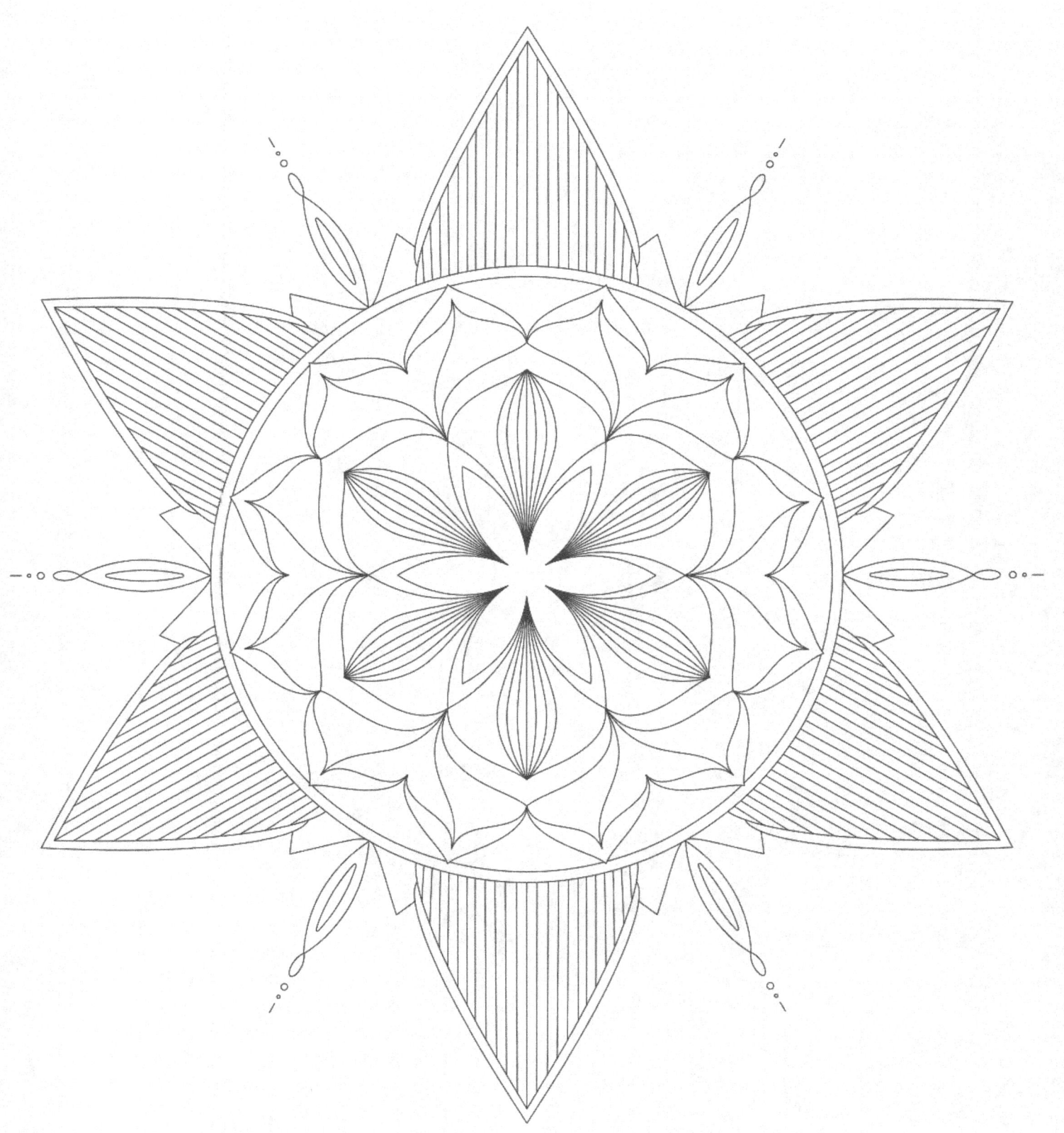

"Let your unique awesomeness and positive energy inspire confidence in others."
Anonymous

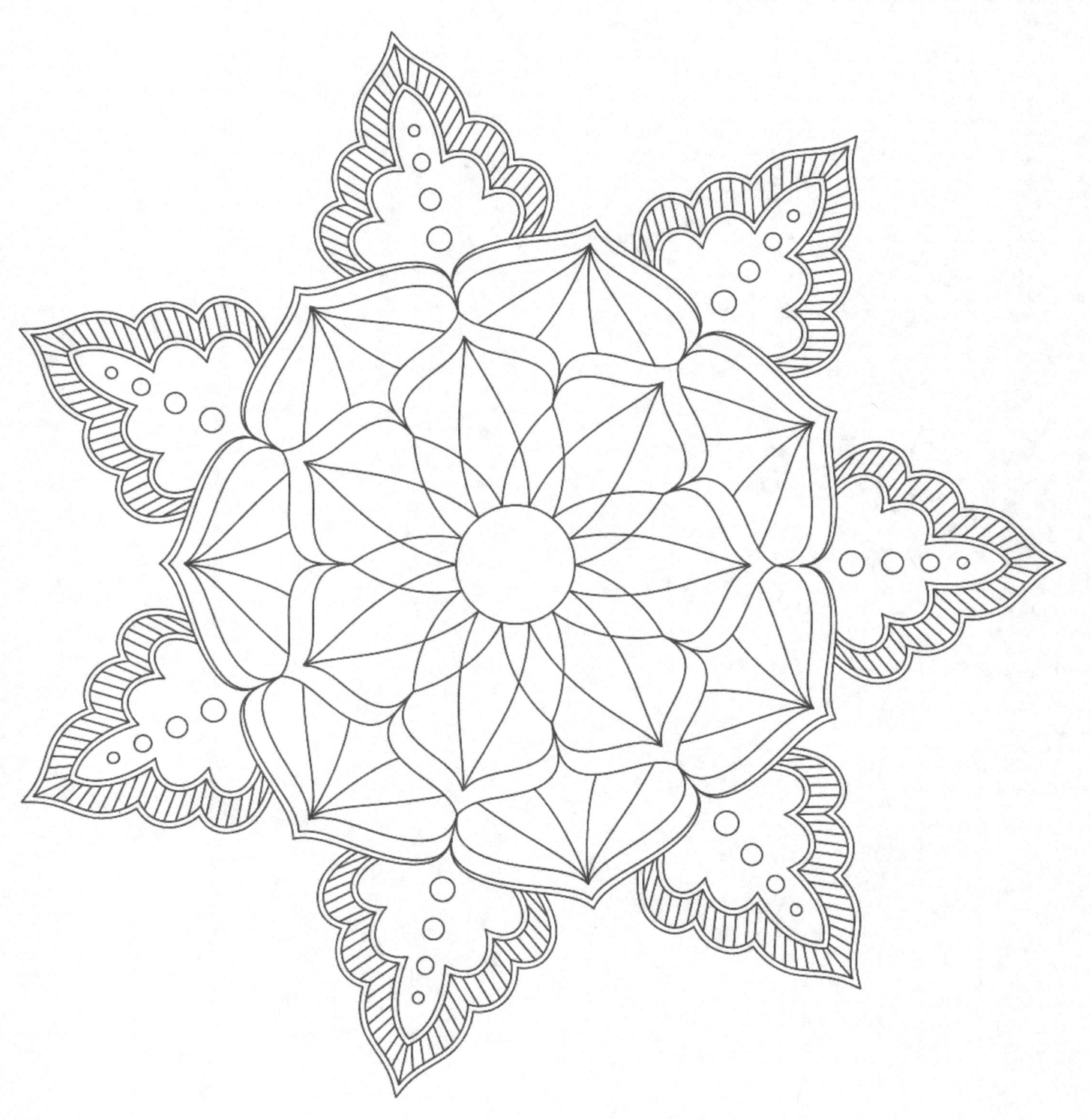

"Wherever you go, no matter what the weather, always bring your own sunshine."
Anthony J. D'Angelo

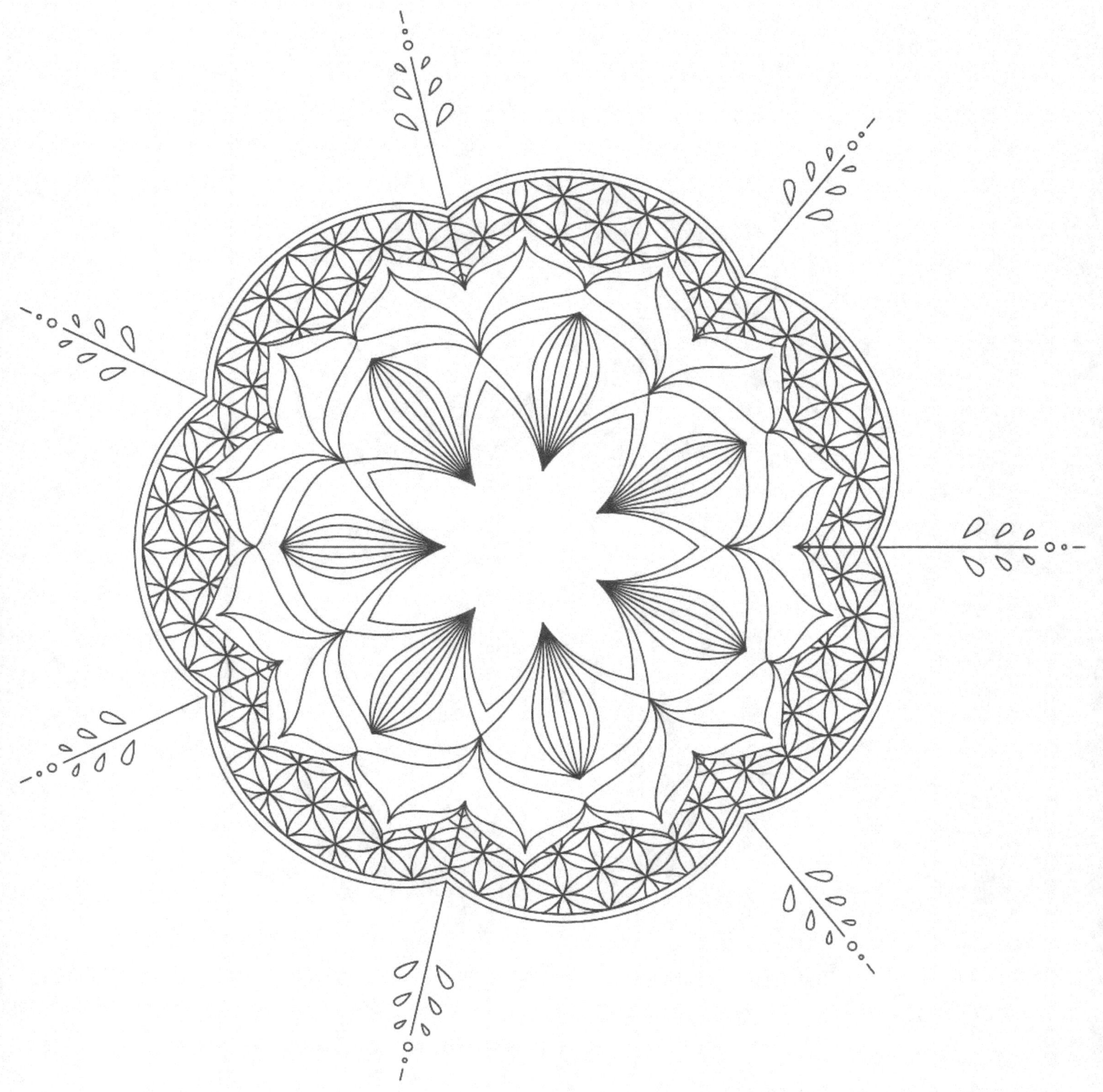

"If you want the light to come into your life, you need to stand where it is shining."
Guy Finley

"Success is the sum of small efforts
repeated day in and day out."
Robert Collier

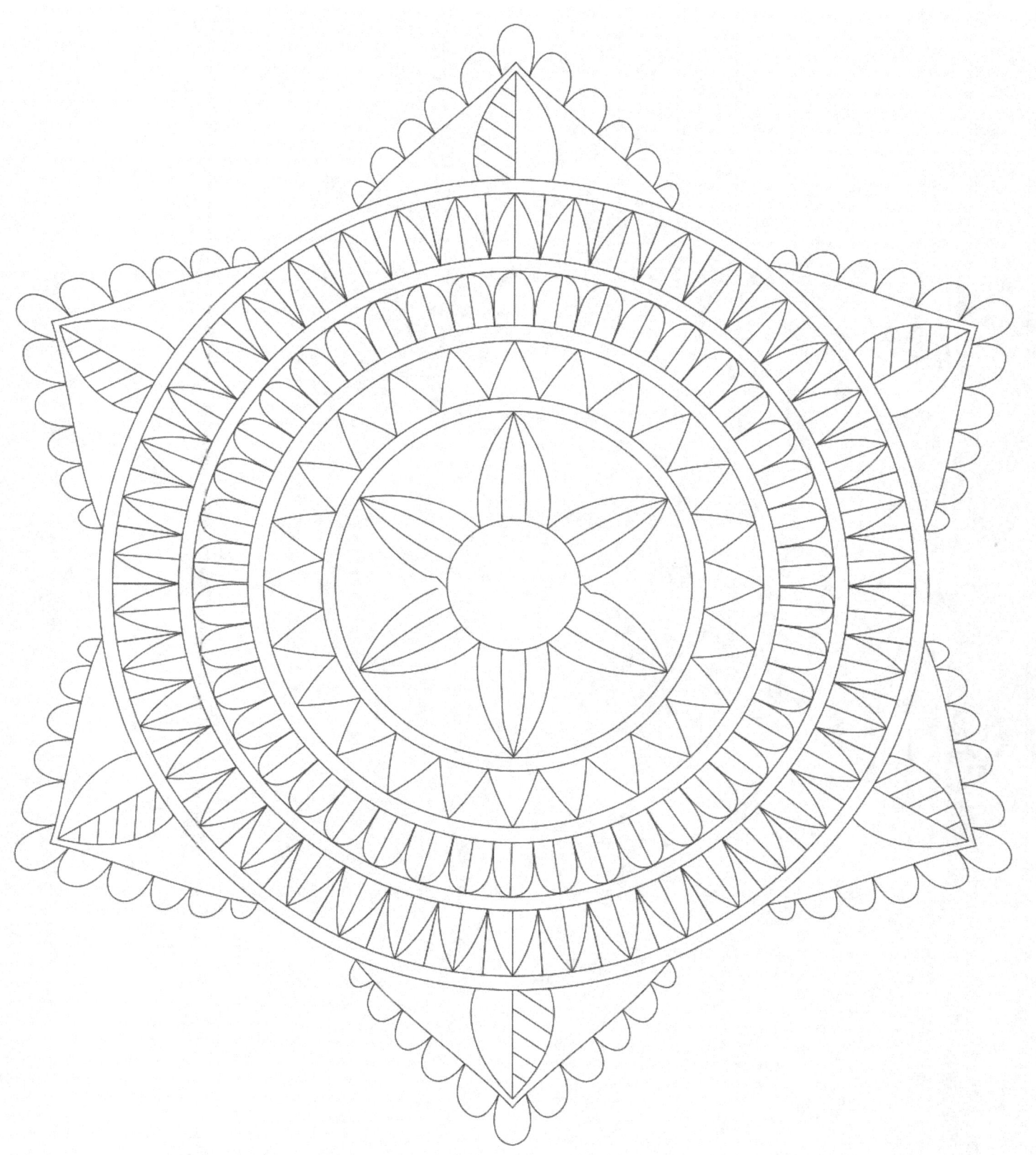

"Success is the sum of small efforts
repeated day in and day out."
Robert Collier

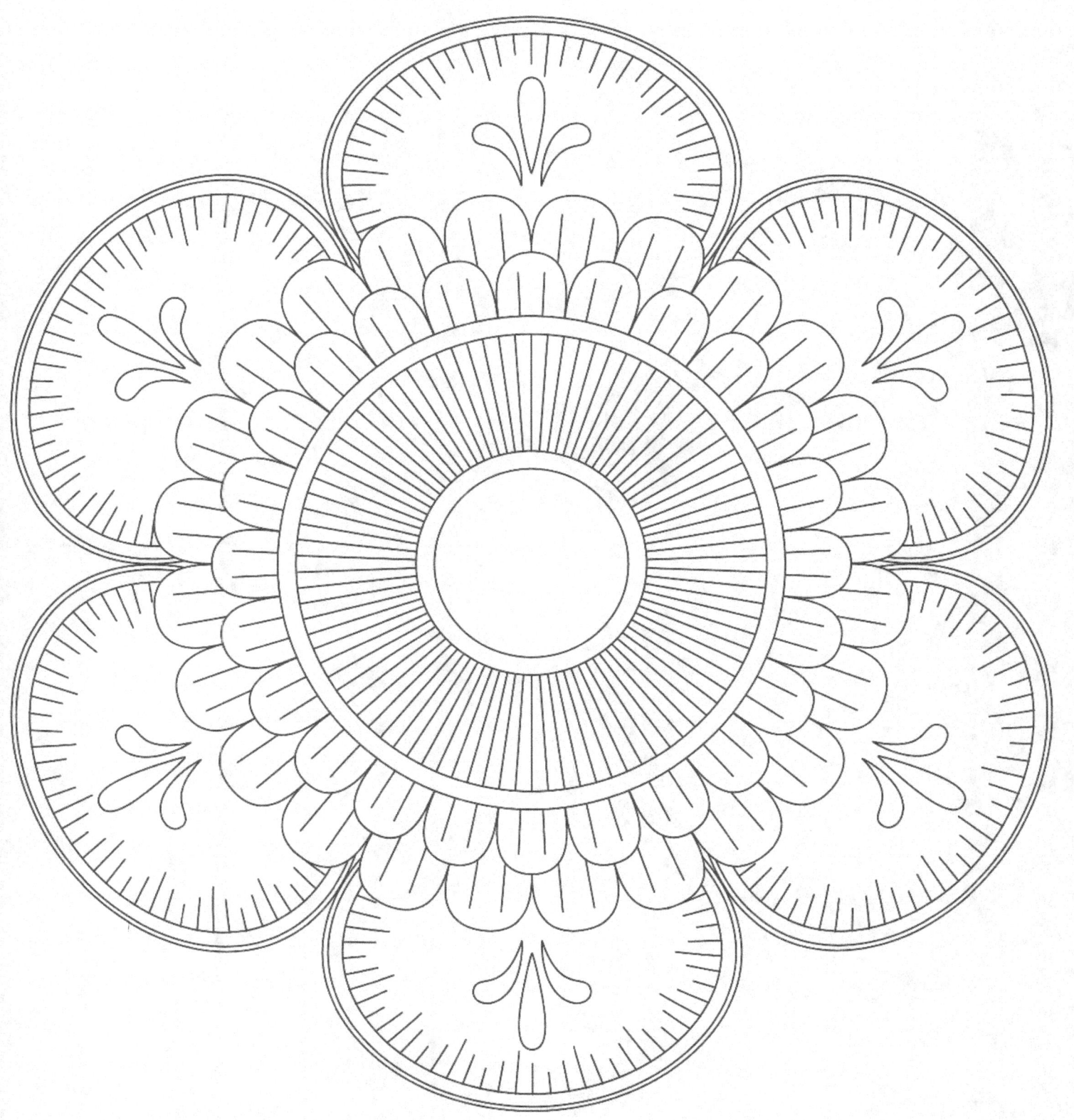

"When we are open to new possibilities, we find them. Be open and skeptical of everything."
Todd Kashdan

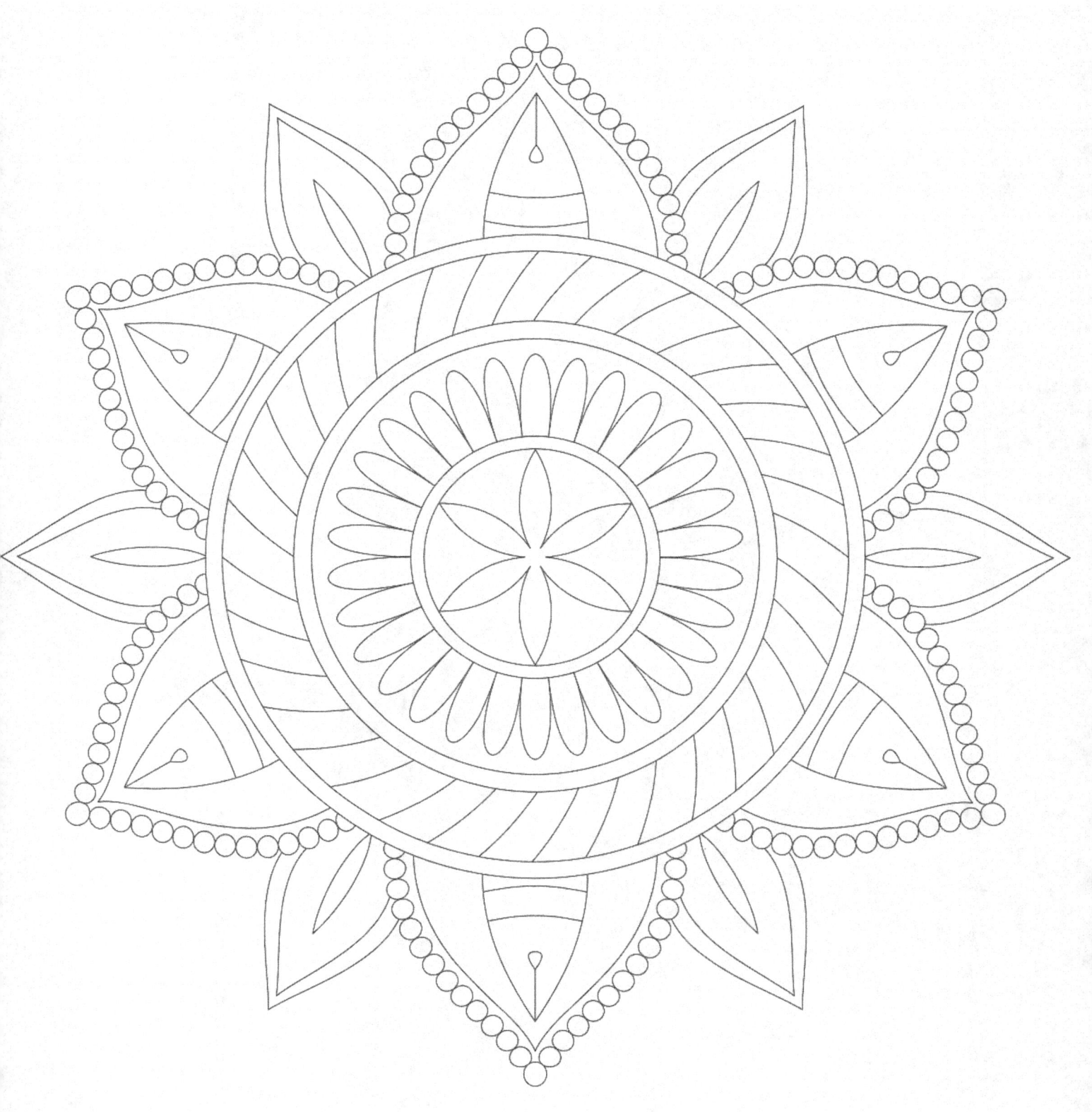

"Happiness is the only thing that multiplies when you share it."
Albert Schweitzer

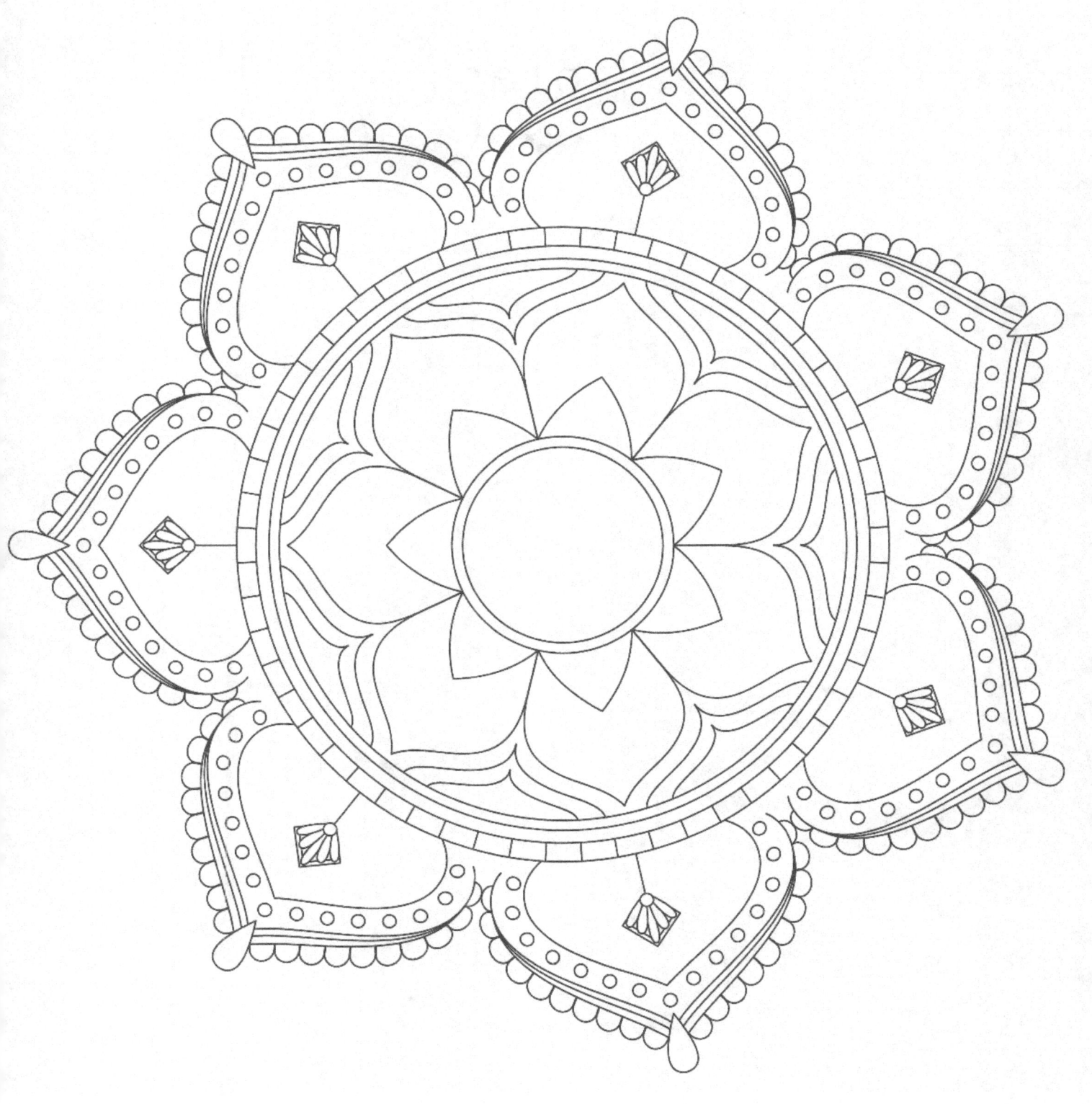

"Do it for yourself. No one will do it for you."
Marggiori Lopez

Notes

Notes

Notes

Notes
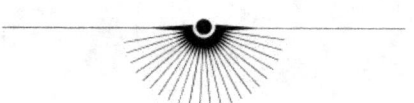

www.ingramcontent.com/pod-product-compliance
Lightning Source LLC
Chambersburg PA
CBHW080614220526
45466CB00010B/3343